A TERMINATION

Also by Honor Moore:

Our Revolution

The Bishop's Daughter

Red Shoes (poems)

Darling (poems)

The White Blackbird

Memoir (poems)

Mourning Pictures (play in poems)

Honor Moore

●

A TERMINATION

A PUBLIC SPACE BOOKS

NEW YORK

A Public Space Books
PO Box B
New York, NY 10159

A Public Space gratefully acknowledges the support of the New York State
Council on the Arts and the individuals, foundations, and corporations
whose contributions have helped to make this book possible.

NEW YORK STATE OF OPPORTUNITY. | Council on the Arts

The names and identifying characteristics of some of the individuals
appearing in the book have been changed to protect their privacy.

Library of Congress Control Number: 2024932803
ISBN: 9798985976922
eISBN: 9798985976939

www.apublicspace.org

987654321

For my nieces, my nephews, and my students
A few things I wanted you to know

A TERMINATION

I Did Not Tell

Not my lover, not my parents, and they said I couldn't tell a friend. I remember my terror that the psychiatrist would not believe me. I'm sure I cried. I'm sure I told him I did not want to marry the father and was certain I could not care for a child. All of this complicated further because I'd unwillingly had sex with a man other than my lover, so I never knew who the father was and there was no way to find out. My lover was one of my professors; in those days, there was no taint of the criminal in such a relationship, nor were they unusual. You could not have persuaded me then that what I felt was not love but a desire to be him, to seize his talent for myself.

But I got pregnant, which I denied until the test came back. I think I must already have known what the results would be when I started to feel oddly happy and found myself standing in the middle of the room, sun pouring through the window, my hands across my belly. The psychiatrist wrote a letter and an obstetrician performed my abortion in a hospital. The month was April, the year 1969.

I

I Stand in the Middle of the Room

I was twenty-three and my hair was long, almost to my waist. A movie camera would take in a lovely young woman. Why have I always been tormented by my weight? I have full breasts, and on this particular morning, they are sensitive to the touch. And perhaps suddenly larger. Did I already know I was pregnant?

I stand in the middle of the room and stroke my belly. I keep refining that image. I am standing in the sun, wearing a cream-colored, silky tunic, my hands are on my belly and I am thinking this: I am proud. Sun, son. I have always believed I would have had a son. Fifty-two years old by now, a physicist or a famous oncologist.

I am trying to picture walking into the hospital that morning. I see myself spin through glass doors, and what comes to me is something medieval—hair shorn, an outcast shamed for her sexual excess, sunlight permanently removed from planet Earth. I always get sad in April. The change of season? I remember no sympathy from my friends, who at the time were mostly young men, but it's possible I never told them I was pregnant. I don't think I knew, one of them said recently.

Standing in the sunny room, my hands on my belly. I still do that sometimes when I am overweight. Hands on the belly as a boast. This is my body, and I have made it.

It's April again and I am sad: *April is the cruellest month* (T. S. Eliot, 1922). Apocalypse within. Not until now do I identify that sadness. I'd thought love led to marriage, pregnancy, motherhood, happiness. The abortion disrupted that inevitability, but I was young and I paid no attention. Paying attention now, I would say the word *sadness* lacks dimension: freedom also, and the fear of being seen.

Seven years later, walking a path drifted with snow, I slip on hidden ice, and as I pull myself up, he calls to me from the porch of his studio: January, an artists' colony. He was beautiful, his body, and my body's response to what we did. He had a house on an island off the coast of Spain and that was where I imagined we would live. I would be barefoot and baking bread, our child wailing, the colors chalky blue and white. My body is smooth and open, my face its ideal, and he would make love to me whenever the child was sleeping. We have many children, went the dream, which gave way to an open sea. Decades later I would spend three weeks on a Greek island with a couple and their first child. Every day we would go to the beach, the baby on a striped blanket. How merciful the sun was on that island. My skin got dark that summer but never burned, and one evening I read my poems for them as the sun set through the windows, turning the room gold.

Thirty years after the slip on the ice, another winter, and there he is in the main hall of the same artists' colony. He says hello, introduces me to the Russian painter he's driven here for a residency. My usual ability to disguise discomfort deserts me, and I cannot summon more than *hello*. Right here, in the place where it happened. The pay phone in its wooden booth is still there; I remembered his voice in my ear, heated and desperate; he'd had to leave early and I stayed out the month, emptied out but young enough to assume this was forever, which of course it was not.

After that surprise encounter, he wrote me that my indifference that day had hurt him terribly. How could I snub him *after what we had*? I made some excuse, not able to remind him that he had gone back to his wife while I had left the man I lived with.

The phone booth was gone the next time I returned to the colony, along with the history carved and inked on the wooden interior—*They all cheat on their wives*, said the older woman poet—various phone numbers, graffiti. And the circle I'd inscribed in purple ink as we talked, over and over outlining the dime I needed to get the operator to charge the call. Don't you understand, the psychiatrist said, that "Ten Cents a Dance" (Rodgers and Hart, 1930) is a song about prostitution?

I kept my blue Corvair in the multistory outdoor parking lot of the building where I lived. Did I drive myself to the hospital? No drugstore pregnancy tests yet, so I must have gone to the gynecologist, a balding older man who wore glasses, whose surname started with *B*, this detail from memory as I kept no journal. I've kept a journal only when I wanted to know and understand what was happening— my mother's death, the era in my life when I returned to men after years of women lovers—but in New Haven at twenty-three, I didn't want to know and understand. I didn't believe in anything I was doing.

I was at drama school training to become an arts administrator. I had proved myself talented at it—summer productions directed by brilliant young men in a small theatre at Harvard, raves in the Boston papers, once even the *New York Times*, though of the young women who supervised and arranged, no mention. The solution was, I thought, graduate school. A degree called an MFA would make what I did glamorous.

There would soon be books praising the rebellion of our generation with titles like *The Greening of America* (Charles A. Reich, 1970), but they were all about the boys. What color green was a girl? (We didn't yet call ourselves women.)

The building where I lived was on York Street, three blocks from the school. Across the street another concrete building housed a supermarket and a café called the Stone Balloon. Joni Mitchell sang there but I didn't go hear her, too scared to be alone. I didn't go hear Leonard Cohen either, that voice singing "Suzanne" (1967) on my new KLH stereo.

Memory now moves me back to college, to one of those parties we always had after opening nights. I'm a freshman living in a dorm. No marijuana yet, but we drank, alcohol purchased by those who were twenty-one. Then I see him— the word I am looking for meant *capture* or *get his attention*—I know Mimi would remember but she's dead now. Would Edie remember? *I had a scene with . . .* A dark room, his smooth, pale face catching the light. Why was it that we found him so sexy? He would jump to his death from an apartment building soon after we graduated. Later, it occurred to me that he must have been gay. Lasting image, he's very drunk, his smile radiant, a garland of grapes on his head. Dionysus.

Someone asks what I'm writing about. Autonomy, I answer, and my abortion, then choke back a surge of the old shame. I had one too, she says. I was not going to let my body take over, goddamn it.

Femaleness. All my life I have been clearing space for it. Or was it claustrophobia? You're in a closed car, fighting to get out.

I try another approach, writing as if to my nieces. I hardly know what you think of me, your never-married aunt. You might recognize me at twenty-one, but only because there's a family resemblance. I have just graduated from college and am staying in Cambridge for the summer to produce a season of plays. I feel an undertow, almost physical, pulling me back. Do you ever feel that way?

Three friends and I have rented a big apartment on Trowbridge Street. I have a secret boyfriend, secret because of the intensity of the sex we are having, my first multiple orgasms, secret because I suspect that the brilliant young men who write and direct do not want me stepping out.

Driving in downtown Boston in snarled traffic: Since then, I cling to it as a metaphor, me in traffic in a blue Corvair. I was finally alone. Important to understand the relief I felt. So much ruckus at home. So much to do at the theatre. So much noise. I am both relieved by solitude and terrified of it.

There were two men who might have made me pregnant. I remember one night drinking in New York with friends, beginning a monologue that flowed as if it had been stored inside me like a long-lost, never-played recording. Are you all right? someone said. I was spinning out a fallback future: drunk, red-faced, obese, married with grown-up children. She dies in late middle age in an automobile accident, possibly suicide.

In a small house in Connecticut, a grand piano, a man playing Chopin. He always gets very drunk at his dinner parties. Jordan and Daisy, he says, addressing two of us on the cream-colored sofa (F. Scott Fitzgerald, *The Great Gatsby*, 1925). Which am I? Neither. Rereading in my fifties, I find myself not in the two women but in Nick Carraway, the narrator. I participate, make jokes, reply, but like him, I hold myself at a distance.

I climb the stairs of the outdoor lot and get into my Corvair. I had not told my parents I was pregnant. Such a fuckup, almost willfully skipping days of birth control pills.

My mother and abortion come into the same frame only when she is advised, pregnant for the sixth time, to have an abortion herself, that her health may otherwise be in danger. She refuses. Each birth was a canto in the epic of her childbearing, and I remember the story of that one: she felt the head sliding out, got herself to the hospital and almost instantly gave birth. My confirmation to the Episcopal Church was the next day, and my mother was not there. I remember the weight of the bishop's hands on my head, as she must always have remembered the solidity of my sister's head emerging from between her legs.

I painted the white bookcase orange enamel and maybe the shelves black. I set its end against the wall so it extends into the room, a boundary between living room and dining room. My apartment in New Haven is the first place I lived by myself. I placed my light-blue Royal typewriter at one end and will sit there to write. My favorite color then was blue, but orange was edging in.

I also had an orange suit, smooth wool and the light-orange color of cantaloupe, with a long jacket I loved because it covered my shameful buttocks. What's that behind you, my mother would say.

I want to stick to my subject, which is consciousness. When did I first smoke dope? Was I stoned when I invented my fallback future? When did we start talking about extending time, extending the duration of time. *Consciousness* and I think of looking at someone more intensely than usual.

If I'd had a son, would he have looked like one of my nephews? I think of him, turning slightly toward me. And into view comes a former student—it was as if he wanted me to be his lover. Can we have a cup of coffee? he said; I'd like to talk to you. Maybe that's how I will come to have a son, in reincarnations. Usually, they are an age that would have them born close to 1969. Why didn't you take him home? said my therapist more than once: a younger man I'd met in a café, the flirtatious waiter in the Indian restaurant two blocks from where I live. I wouldn't do that, I said.

Diapers, and my mother trying to figure out a more efficient method—Pampers not yet in existence—dirty cloth diapers put in a drawstring bag to be picked up, a new batch delivered. Jab a safety pin first through one side of the diaper, then the other. Oh the softness of their skin: the smell of

Desitin still makes me faint—it came in a tube like toothpaste; it signified clean, though the fragrance of baby excrement was not unpleasant.

The phone ringing, the doorbell ringing, a child shouting or weeping, the cleaning woman, the repairman, someone from the church. My mother spent her life distracted. A wave of noise slowing and fading out. I wanted quiet. When I managed to be alone, I was happy. An early quiet—one of the bathrooms in my grandmother's enormous house, a very large tub with wide, silvery spouts, the soft sound of water rushing, then it's full, the water aqua. You look out the window to green fields, the Guernsey cows with their rust-brown-and-white coats. I have a black-and-white snapshot of two of them in a field there, in a silver picture frame. In the distance, the dairy where milk and heavy cream were bottled, butter churned, cottage cheese cultured and strained.

I tell my grandmother about my apartment and ask her if she has an extra bed and she sends one, brass, from the governess's bedroom. I ask her for a rug and she says, Go buy one you like and I'll pay for it. I didn't know where to go for a Persian rug like the ones she had, so I went to Greenwich Village and bought a Navajo one that was too small. I asked for a clock and she sent me an awful modern brass one. She didn't know I was lonely for old and precious things.

One day in college, I decided to be happy. I woke up sad and looked in the mirror over the bureau and smiled at myself. Good morning. Good morning. I'd smile back at myself and then go to breakfast in the dorm. It was something I told friends about, a mirror trick.

Diet pills were my mother's idea. She didn't like what was happening to my body, breasts, bottom. Small orange pills and I'd have no appetite. My mother did not menstruate until the age of sixteen, was "flat chested" until she had children. It was she who wanted nine of us, eighty-one months of her body's life. Big, small. Fat, thin. Would her body ever return to normal? A decade after her final child was born, she put herself on an early version of the Atkins diet—high protein, no carbohydrates. I have always associated rare hamburger with the cancer that killed her.

I keep the pills on top of the orange bookcase. I run out of them, and my mood plummets. I did not want to be estranged from how I really felt, I thought, so I went off of them cold turkey and told no one. For days, I felt so heavy I could hardly get up from a chair, so far down, I thought I would die. It was during about then that I lost the gold pin, textured and set with tiny sapphires and rubies, that my aunt, my godmother, had given me. I had worn it on the apricot suit with the long jacket.

Once, in my sixties, on a massage table I hallucinated myself within my mother. Her vagina had a narrow opening, its walls were dry and stiff, and I couldn't get out. I believe that my skull was slightly distorted in shape at birth. You can see it still, the opening for my right eye slightly smaller than the left, the right side of my face slightly compressed. I think it contributed to the headaches.

It has always been that way, my father would say in a tender tone of voice. Your face has an asymmetry I like, said the older European woman photographer when I was in my forties.

It's the summer I graduated from college. The large living room of a second-floor apartment on Mount Auburn Street. Empty coffee-stained paper cups and vodka bottles, stench of cigarette smoke. A classmate and I, both women, have arrived as arranged, expecting pages of the script, and he is making excuses. Tomorrow, he declares. The season will open with his translation of Aristophanes's *Peace*. The year is 1967 and the draft is on, now thirty-five thousand recruits per month.

Often we'd pull him from his bed: Okay, okay, okay. Not vodka, I now remember, but rum and Coke. He drank too much, but he was the engine of our theatrical endeavors, redeemed by talent, excoriating wit, charisma, his status as a brilliant young man. He got sentimental like any drunk, but I was still scared of him. I had ways of dealing with the fear: I folded it up and placed it on the shelf where I kept the perfectly adequate dimensions of my real self—she had no language, the fear was chartreuse, acid green.

He was my first gynophobe. He made unpleasant allusions to the female anatomy and coached actresses as if they were strippers. *Give it all you got, baby. That's it. Come to Daddy.* He had unerring intuition, got what he needed in a performance by verbal assault, insult, flattery, and seduction. I enabled him. All the women did, I want to say; now I see that we were two kinds of women. Those of us who were at Radcliffe or in for the summer from Vassar. And girlfriends or one-night stands recruited in Boston bars, he seduced into costume design, bed, or both. Such a snob. I had nothing but contempt for those women.

I am Margaret Fuller and I accept the universe. Words of a play I saw in the early 1970s (Megan Terry, *Calm Down Mother*), the first ever I saw by a woman of my generation. The actress had red hair.

I have never forgotten her, a large awkward woman with coppery hair alone on the stage: *I am Margaret Fuller and I accept the universe.*

II

Intercourse Is a Straight Line, and Dry

Two tall people, the man on top. Sex is curved and moist and in the dark. Intercourse is military and required. Intercourse is scheduled. Intercourse does not require love. What my parents called *intercourse*, we called in high school *going all the way*. The phrase had a tinge of sin. We did not say *we had sex*, a phrase tinged with routine. My mother talked about birth control, and she and my father practiced it. She used a diaphragm and later was on the pill. I think only one of her nine pregnancies was unplanned, and that she had one or two miscarriages. I was in college when I lost my virginity.

Birth control was the phrase.

Sex—you may not love the partner "as a person," but your body loves theirs. I like the bringing of morning coffee by my lover to the bed; in movies and on television what arouses

me is not health club bathrobe begarbed sunshine sex, but—
and I do not choose this—what is forbidden, even violent.

I learned that children arrived as a consequence of intercourse—Do you know how a woman gets pregnant, sweetie?—
nothing about pleasure. When my parents expressed their
love, they spoke in the badinage of their youth, with a kind
of sarcastic affection I did not associate with physical contact
or my mother's pregnant body. This was before I knew the
word *erotic*. Before I read "I Sing the Body Electric" (Walt
Whitman, 1855), years before "You Turn Me On, I'm a
Radio" (Joni Mitchell, 1972).

In the dark of a car after a Saturday night movie (*Lawrence of
Arabia*, 1962), I get seriously *turned on* for the first time. I am
quite sure the boy with whom I was *making out* was frightened
to feel what he was feeling; he snubbed me in Greek class
at 8:15 Monday morning, and the silent treatment went on
for weeks. What was supposed to be a triumph was a failure.

Recently, I streamed a television miniseries about a high
school teacher, a woman, falling in love with her student.
They have a passionate affair, are discovered, and she is pros-
ecuted and incarcerated. In the tenth episode, the denoue-
ment, which takes place after she is released from prison a

decade after the fact, he tells her that their affair destroyed his life, and she apologizes. Okay, but was there no love? Why would the filmmakers deny the love they were at such pains to depict?

And now returns the professor with whom I had an affair in graduate school, the man by whom I probably became pregnant, and then, unaccountably, Wyoming, the image of a vast shallow crater once a lake, trace of prehistory now a scrub plain. You spend the rest of your life trying to recover from the anger. My love for that professor, whom I'll call L, is the first of the loves I hang on to past plausibility.

I am in Wyoming, staying on a stretch of green at the edge of the crater. It's afternoon, and a flock of wild turkeys walk ahead of me, gobbling. The birds are in shadow. I am in the eighth year of an on-and-off affair with a man whose marriage was always breaking up, or so I keep believing. You can call back this afternoon if you want, he says on the phone. *If you want*. I understood finally. I never called him again.

Since then I have been unable to fall in love, every such feeling a false start. I recently ran into that man, my last great love. We were at a crowded party walking in opposite directions, and he was with his new wife, a woman half his age. I didn't know her, but I had met her once. Instead of greeting me with a smile as he always had, he pushed me out of the way with his elbow.

I wonder what my life would have been if I had considered my virginity as precious as the act of sex?

I'm thinking that question is an entrance into philosophy, meaning the area of thought that considers the body versus the soul, desire versus sin. I don't understand, says my exasperated lover, you think sex is holy or something. Certainly miraculous. Dorothy Day (1897–1980) converted to Christianity and became a Catholic when she gave birth to her daughter. How did she feel about sex? Miracles interfere with philosophy, the way desire does.

He is poised above me, as if in a push up. I want us to be naked and him to fall into me. I am a freshman in college, still a virgin. I remember an actual vibration between our bodies. I want to say yes, but I say no, not unless I am "special" to him. He pursues me to my summer job, but by then I am onto someone else.

In my mother's bathroom—a small white rubber circle within a flexible white wire hoop encased in rubber, or perhaps plastic. Once, when I was about six, I mistook a tube of the sperm-killing gel for toothpaste, which was why I recognized the smell when I got my own.

The task of birth control was entirely mine. I found a doctor whose office was on Fifth Avenue—I remember crossing the street, in view of Saint Patrick's Cathedral, where God enforced the chastity of Catholic women, a prohibition that overflowed to Protestants like myself. I told the doctor that I was in love with my boyfriend and wanted to have "intercourse" with him; perhaps I even said we were engaged. The doctor, who seemed older than my parents, told me that to have sexual intercourse before marriage was not in my "worldview." In view was a summer in New York City. I roomed with two friends to keep secret that I spent nights in the apartment my boyfriend rented on Riverside Drive and 108th Street, a window seat overlooking the Hudson River where he read me e. e. cummings ("anyone lived in a pretty how town," 1940). I took art classes and he worked in a bank. The plan was to dispense with my virginity. He was the one I was going to marry.

The second doctor I went to did prescribe, and I acquired the apparatus and the necessary gel. But if the boyfriend and I were destined to enjoy ourselves in bed, the mechanics of intercourse, the diaphragm, and the stench of the gel were effective in preventing us from doing so.

I spent every possible weekend that fall with him in New York City until he enlisted in the Marines and broke up with me. I was inconsolable. We reconciled through letters, but when he returned on leave that summer, my desire had gone blank and moved on. He came to the house my mother had rented at the seashore north of Boston. At dark we went for a walk on the beach and he tried to kiss me but I couldn't and he left. The next morning a friend of my mother's came to photograph each of her nine children. I could never look at the portrait, such smiles on the faces of my sisters and brothers, such wistful loss on mine.

Moved on to what? Perhaps I was reading Ruth Benedict (*Patterns of Culture*, 1934), perhaps a bloody play by John Webster (ca. 1580–ca. 1625). A tall man with glasses approaches me in the library, a graduate student in philosophy, he says.

What was he doing in the Radcliffe library? Looking for the likes of me. Very quickly we were sleeping together. I go to the theatre and work, come home for supper he cooks for me and time in bed.

Music on the radio began to matter that summer, a soundtrack for this new self who came into existence when I left the theatre for the philosopher's apartment. I was waiting for a green light at Mass. Ave. in my blue Corvair, the radio blasting a song called "A Whiter Shade of Pale" (Procol Harum, 1967), which seemed to describe the too-white body I was trying so hard to accept. And then, in that bed pushed up against a shelf of philosophy books, I began to have orgasms; this was a new body I couldn't get enough of. Even if I could have put it into words, there was no one I could talk to about the split I felt between the narrow bed and the theatre where my job was to get people to work hard for no money, to put on the plays we all believed in, which audiences would flock to.

As soon as he opened the door, the philosopher said, Listen to this! He held up an album called *Pet Sounds* (the Beach Boys, 1966) and then played it: *Wouldn't it be nice to live together?* I thought it would be nice, but not with him. Because of those cascading, abundant, and utterly disorienting orgasms? Yes. He kept smiling and cooking for me and trying to get me to take a night off, to rest. I couldn't understand it, someone taking care of me. He was the only child of parents who were academics; it was their apartment; they were in Nova Scotia for the summer.

What was I using for birth control? Still the diaphragm or was I already on the pill? I don't remember inserting the diaphragm so I must have been on the pill.

Suddenly, I was freed from my mother's hectoring about my body, my rear end, my breasts, my weight. It was as if I had new skin, new hair, new insides. What had been an object of my contempt now became a means of ecstasy. Had the philosopher been capable of love, I might have been happy from then on. Was I capable of love? You assume he broke it off, but it was me. I seduced his best friend. Ironic, what I find myself writing next is that it didn't seem proper to have all that sex. What I mean is, all that pleasure.

She never married, my great-uncle said. *Never married*, a formulaic epithet that conjured not only old women dressed in black, white lace caps covering their hair, but certain women of his generation, "mannish" in trousers and well-tailored jackets. *Sapphist* was the word he might have used had he spoken further of the lovers and friends of his sister, my mother's mother, Margarett. He'd never say he disapproved of her, only that, like Cleopatra, she had "immortal longings" (William Shakespeare, *Antony and Cleopatra*, 1607).

What would he have said of me? She never married. She wrote books.

Adeline Walker worked at Eli Lilly and Company as an executive secretary, and she was the most interesting of our babysitters when we lived in Indianapolis, turning up in fashionable suits to sit with us at supper. She was my first "career woman." I was enthralled by the musical lilt of her conversation, but I don't remember what we talked about, only that my questions made her laugh. There was space around her, I might have said if I'd tried to articulate it. What I would have meant was that she seemed *independent*. In Manhattan in the 1980s, I saw her again, now Sister Andrea and dressed in the habit of an Episcopal order of nuns. She had become a mother superior. Her laugh, always easy, was easier still. At the time I considered nuns protofeminists and assumed many of them lovers with one another. I wondered if Sister Andrea loved women.

Honor doesn't need a husband, M, a high school friend, declared. We were in our twenties. Her use of the third person made it conclusive: I had money so I didn't need to marry, at least not for practical reasons. Her husband was not rich. Did she mean I could live comfortably on one income? Or that I didn't have to work? I always worked, but for years felt guilty if I earned—until I could no longer afford "anything I wanted."

Decades later, on a visit to Indianapolis to publicize a book, I complimented another high school friend on her husband and asked their story. I didn't say yes, she said; I didn't sleep with him or anyone until I was married. An admission of bestiality would not have shocked me more, but her means got her a lovely husband and a pair of twins. Mine got me the single life.

III

Don't Come Home Pregnant

I chose apple green for the sofa, a convertible one so I could have overnight guests. Beatrice, an acquaintance from college, by coincidence moved in upstairs. She was mysterious about her personal life. I envied her efficient intelligence, her beauty, and her very good figure. I did not trust her.

After the philosopher, a rampage, sleeping with as many men as I could. That spring the college had summoned a consultant to "talk to us" about sex. My roommates and I thought the young man in the ill-fitting suit ridiculous, though I doubt we would have been more sympathetic to a woman—no feminism yet. What constitutes promiscuity? I asked to start the conversation. He hesitated. Ten partners, he replied. I took it as a challenge, I declared out loud. Beatrice was more discreet.

She had a studio apartment with a parquet floor. The floor of my one-bedroom was white linoleum tile. Beatrice knew she wanted to be an architect and lived as if she were perching; I hung curtains. My third day in New Haven, she arrived at my door with the very handsome son of a famous American writer, who did not speak. She didn't like him much, she said later. That was the thing about Beatrice, she didn't like anyone much. What I failed to understand was that she didn't like me much either.

There was a split between what I was doing in daylight and what I wanted to be doing.

As an architecture student, Beatrice was drawing plans for buildings; I was tearing tickets for the Yale Rep's mawkish production of *'Tis Pity She's a Whore*, a Jacobean tragedy about incest by John Ford (1586–ca. 1639). I had tickets to the New York Film Festival, which I had to give away. I did not think to ask to be excused. Another me might have gotten into her blue Corvair and hit the interstate for Lincoln Center.

I looked for myself in the mirror, scrutinizing every angle of my face. I began to write on the pale-blue typewriter at the blue table. A secret until my second year when, having supper one night with two third-year friends, one a playwright and one a director, both men, I made an announcement: I want to write. No crash of cymbals, no thunderous applause: Well, go ahead and write, said the playwright. Maybe you'll write forever, said the director. He had a small laugh and told Buddhist stories that hinged on a shrug at mortality.

It's 1969, my second year at the school, and I am almost pregnant. The marriage of my friend Bob had disintegrated and he had no way to pay for a divorce. I offered to go to Mexico with him and pay for the flight, so off we went to Juárez, where we walked a hot, crowded strip to a doorway that matched the address Bob had on a scrap of paper. We climbed stairs to a crowded office, and he made the necessary arrangements. We stayed around a few days to get a document pronouncing him single. We were not lovers but friends, and I always thought him the most talented writer I met at the school. After Juárez, we went to Mexico City, where by chance we ran into a drama school friend named Ting—was his wife with him?

From Mexico City we drove to Mérida, where I put us up in an elegant hotel. Nothing was expensive. We ate roast pork, never to be surpassed in tenderness and flavor.

At the market, I went mad for those blouses, white with embroidery at the neckline, which I wore as minidresses. We began to yearn for a beach, so we took a tiny plane to Isla Mujeres, but it was off-season and rainy. We left after a day.

The photographer, a design student, asked me to model in the nude. It did not occur to me that there was anything to fear, and I was curious. I thought of Edward Weston's gorgeous photographs of Tina Modotti (1924) and imagined that seeing my body in black and white might counter my belief that I was not beautiful.

The birth control pills I was taking came in a flat plastic dispenser with numbered slots that helped you keep track of your cycle—C-Quens (Eli Lilly, discontinued 1970). The sell was that you felt less bovine, the innovation that the amount of hormone in a pill mimicked the natural cycle, lessening as the month progressed. I hate the word *cycle*; it feels like restraint.

I am twenty-one, twenty-two, twenty-three, and I am taking birth control pills so I won't get pregnant. The subterranean blue and green of me, some undercurrent of electrical will, surge of becoming myself, sometimes simply skipped the pill. Now there are eye drops I must take in order not to go blind: Some mornings I just look at them and the synapse that says take them doesn't fire, so I don't.

I climb the curved stone stairs to L's campus apartment.

I place myself in my apartment on York Street, front-facing view onto the street, sliding glass doors, floor-to-ceiling curtains—I'd had them made, blue, orange—oh, and what was the other color, I don't know. Ocher? Why the extravagance of curtains? Make myself a home. I scan the space. I look over at the blue Parsons table. Clever to ask my father for a dining room table. About having my own money: I was unconscious that people would hate me for it and so I didn't hide it. Why did no one warn me about that?

This is what I see: almost twenty-two, the dress Italian and sleeveless, layers of lavender crepe with a pattern. The welcoming reception is on the bare stage of the drama school theatre, paint-scarred floor, bare bulb lighting, drinks in paper cups.

At such parties in college, I'd be talking about Russian poetry or the wildness of English Jacobean plays like *The Duchess of Malfi* (John Webster, 1613). Who should play the duchess? The air like a fine clear oil; perhaps it has a faint fragrance—in the 1990s the British apothecary Neal's Yard

Remedies popularized a scent called Geranium—that scent, but so faint I breathe almost without smelling it.

I don't think of breathing as I dress for that first party at the drama school, the lovely crepe dress I think of as normal length, by which I mean normal *for the time*. I look at photos and see myself in shockingly short skirts and think, How short was that Italian dress that I remember as modest?

You must be an actress, says the directing student who later said, Maybe you'll write forever.

No, I'm in administration.

I also met Gordon that night, tipsy, smiling, rosy faced, the chair of directing. I remember no one else, but because of the bare stage, everything seemed familiar. A question intrudes from the present. Did you feel safe? I had not felt unsafe since third grade when my only friend ran away so I got lost on the way home from school.

In the kitchen this morning, I was thinking about her narrow wrists, her putting on then taking off rings, earrings, necklaces, bracelets, a friend now suffering a dire cancer. She looked at me one day last summer as we sat outside, out of the blue said, Have you been lonely? I trusted her enough to say yes, which shocked me, because only recently had I ever thought of myself as lonely. The door opens, and her husband, recovering from a terrible fall in which he broke his pelvis and legs, comes out to say hello and waters the red geraniums in the terra-cotta urn. *Urn* is the wrong word. I see him walk toward the plant, then bend and extend his arm to check the earth for moisture.

It's fine, he says, about the plant.

Thank you, darling, she says.

Still in the kitchen, I stop as I prepare my second cup of coffee and am suddenly in tears. The moment resembles a recognition, the scene in a play when one stumbles toward another, her gait changing when she sees herself acknowledged.

Sweetie? My mother's voice, and then memory of the first winter in that grown-up apartment: this was my new life. I scan the room and realize I am looking for my mother, which makes me think that she never visited me in New Haven. My father visited once a month. He had business at the university and would take me out for supper and to the movies. We saw *Bonnie and Clyde* (1967) after hamburgers in a place he remembered from college.

I know Paul Schmidt, I say to Gordon. It was Paul with whom I discussed Russian poetry; maybe Gordon would be that kind of friend. Oh, Paul Schmidt, he says. I should have gone to a place where I already had friends. I was used to having a part in things, some importance in what was being made.

The rabbit test results come by phone.

My psychiatrist specializes in children, and the room where we meet is filled with toys. He seems to be an expert at not connecting, which doesn't bother me. I believed in lack of authentic connection as a remedy. Why did I go to a psychiatrist? Impossible to find a woman psychiatrist, and if you found one she would be a freak, or that is what I thought.

When the rabbit results came, I went back to the older psychiatrist who had referred me to the psychiatrist with toys and tell him I am pregnant.

I remember the shadowy office, his kindly face—*kindly*, I use the word on purpose. I must have hidden my embarrassment that I didn't know what man had made me pregnant, and I don't think the kindly psychiatrist pushed. I must have said I was sure I'd go crazy if I had a baby, since that's what I assumed you needed to say to get what was called a therapeutic abortion. I must also have said I didn't want to tell my parents and that I hadn't told the child psychiatrist because he had an Italian name and so I assumed he was Catholic and therefore against abortion. The kindly psychiatrist reassured me and sent me back to the quiet Italian man in the room of toys, who said that his religion, whatever it was, did not affect what he did as a doctor. Decades later I met the kindly psychiatrist by chance and thanked him for saving my life.

In 1969, all abortions were illegal in Connecticut except in cases where having a child would threaten the life of the mother. Those procedures were considered "therapeutic" and were often performed in hospitals. I had learned over the grapevine that such terminations were the only way to avoid the various back alleys and self-inflicted methods but much more expensive than the going rate, which I remember as six hundred dollars. I would later hear of other alternatives: a New York dentist with a sideline; a progressive gynecologist who worked in a back room; a doctor who set up in a home office.

And this: Just as I was trying not to "come home pregnant," young women activists in Chicago were constructing an underground network to provide safe abortions, not only for privileged women like me but for women who could not afford a therapeutic abortion. At first the procedures were performed at reasonable rates by sympathetic doctors; later a doctor trained the women to perform the operations themselves. From 1968 until the passage of *Roe v. Wade* in 1973, the Jane Collective provided fifteen thousand safe abortions.

The psychiatrist with the Italian name handed me—what?—a letter providing legal means for the termination of my pregnancy? I call the gynecologist and make an appointment. I go to see him. I hand him the piece of paper.

Because I was in the theatre, I make this a play: A bare stage because I have no details. At center in a pool of light, the gynecologist at his desk. Even in his office he is dressed in white. You can't see the pen he holds, but you can see that his hand is poised—as if frozen in time, I say to the actor. A young woman enters from stage left. The lighting is such that you see her come into view; the effect is that the closer she comes to the gynecologist at his desk, the more intense the light. He stands and gestures to the chair and she sits down. They don't speak. As if in a dream, I say to the lighting designer. The young woman hands him a small white square of paper. There is a slow revolve and we see her sitting on the examination table, the doctor standing. She swivels her body and lies down, white sheet a sudden tent over her bent knees, her feet in the metal stirrups. He bends to look in.

It comes to me now that right then, the gynecologist asks again if I want to do this, and I say yes. Did you waver? asks a voice in my head. I want to say no, and that is correct. I did not waver.

Are you sure?

Yes.

Have you told anyone?

No.

It amazes me I didn't tell anyone. I made the decision by myself. But also with the remote-control help of my mother: *Don't come home pregnant.*

My father was twenty-three when he came home wounded—shrapnel through his chest at the Battle of Guadalcanal (November 1942). Three months in a New Zealand hospital: I damn near died. I was twenty-three when I spent one night in a hospital where a man I did not know scraped from my womb the viscera of my body's first bout with reproduction. My only bout with reproduction.

L was born in 1927, eight years after my father, eighteen years before me. He was magical, funny, mercurial, and a Jew. A great love had died young from cancer. I want to say her name was Jane. He drank good wine, I noticed, and he wore Italian cashmere turtleneck sweaters. His hips were narrow, the Italian trousers. He had spent a year in Italy on a Fulbright. He knew Latin and Greek, languages I had studied and loved. He had a musical sense of language. His idea of fun was to rhyme in real life; once when he got a check from his agent, he sent her a telegram: Thank you, you lovely bank, you. He wrote poems and lyrics, operas and plays. He was of the age of abstract expressionism and went often to the Cedar Tavern. He was of the age of jazz, had been present at the Five Spot when Billie Holiday sang, maybe the same night Frank O'Hara listened *while she whispered a song along the keyboard / to Mal Waldron* . . . ("The Day Lady Died," 1964). The first year I was at the school, he was a presence, but not, I think, anyone I knew.

By late June, I'm in the Berkshires, my first real job, a theatre where the very famous of New York and Hollywood perform away from it all. I was the press agent—make friends with the performers so they will consent to the glare of publicity they say they want to avoid. I knew about the funny dark-haired woman because my parents listened to the records she made with a funny man with reddish-blond hair, who one night stood in the back and watched the play she had written and was starring in (Nichols and May, 1959–1962). She was brittle and scary, so how could I say hello? What I said was that I went to the drama school and she asked if I knew a friend of hers named L: Say hello.

When I get back to school: I have a hello for you, I said and saw myself come into focus in his brown eyes. It begins then. An exit from passivity but also an entrance into it—if I could get back all the hours I've spent sitting and waiting by the telephone. I did not say: I want you.

What is "falling in love" language for? I strike off anything to do with love. I first felt it as a force that suggested it would dissolve if coupled with its object. I believed love had meaning and that what I called "passion" was the entrance to it.

I saw the face of God, he says. These are the years of AIDS, and his lover had died. Like me, he has been single. For him, as for me, the poems he writes document desire. In the face of his beloved, at climax, he beholds the face of God. He says this matter of factly, as if he assumes I understand what he means.

In Los Angeles, I read a new poem in a large gallery crowded with women, and afterward, Emily, a friend since college, comes toward me: You have written a great poem. And so I was not alone. Many of the other women in the room were lovers of women, and by then perhaps I was, but the poem tracked my desire for a particular man, the man I met slipping on the ice at the artists' colony.

Like a scraped knee, only inside you, was the image I came up with. Nothing like the pain I sometimes feel in the middle of the night or early this morning, hours before I want to wake up, an ache in the right side of my head, down my right side, a clench half down the back, then tension in the lower back, right hip. A woman in her seventies, alone, much of her life behind her. I take a pill.

No matter how many times I did the math, I could not figure out who made me pregnant.

It must have been after the play I directed. The set was the outline of a cube, thin lengths of wood, unpainted. After seeing it the first night, the dean said it was "sensitive work"— one girl directing a play by another girl. He would not have used the phrase "young woman" and I would not have either. It could be so much better, L said of our perfect thing.

The playwright, honey blond, giggly and wildly talented. She would laugh when she said she grew up in Levittown. She and L, both from New York and both Jews, competed to distill a humor that excluded me; her sensibility had already evolved, whereas whatever gift I had was only just emerging. I saw myself in the play's protagonist, heard myself in the voice of the girl from Levittown, and that enabled me to bring the story of the young woman to life. The title of the play was *The Juncture of Billie Mapes.* L was the worshiped muse of the girl from Levittown, who outlined her eyes in kohl. I, an inheritor of minor WASP money.

Unsaid was that we were both in love with L.

The two of us tidied up after the party—she went home. I wanted L to tell me something about my work on the play, but what he said was that he wanted me to "help" him. I thought he meant with the dishes. No, I think now, with my money.

I was in love with his curly nickel-shiny hair.

Are we an item? he asked in the morning.

No one else had wanted to direct the play by the girl from Levittown. Opening night, the performance, like a phrase of Debussy, caught on the air. What Billie the heroine received was her voice. The girl from Levittown and the girl from old WASP money found that voice together. The evening is a success, a crowd in darkness clapping, writer and director called to the stage.

Their bodies divided them is the sentence I want to write, but the truth is harsher. I betrayed her for a man, set her aside. It is something I regret.

Think of their vision instead, the one they made together, as firm as a wet beach, and think of desire as a thin spill of ocean, tide sinking into the porous sand. It's gray, where things begin.

This is the moment in which, if I'd been a person in authority, I would have asked the administration student experimenting with direction what the experience had been for her. I would have asked if she would like to try studying directing, or writing. *Sensitive work*, it turned out, was not quite acknowledgment. Because her direction of the play was not recognized as achievement, the fact that she had made something kept slipping her mind.

That spring, the girl from money wrote a poem that began "I'm just a midwestern gypsy." She had a crush on a third-year set designer who she imagined might free her from the decadence of L. I'm thinking she was actually finished with L, by then. The play on the main stage was *Coriolanus*, and somehow she was backstage, handing Aufidius his sword.

She went to see the dean one morning. She had started to write, she told him. It seems ridiculous given *sensitive work*, but she was certain he would be receptive. Instead he looked at her from his side of the desk and said, Therapeutic writing isn't always the best.

I was twenty-three and I was asking to be seen as who I was actually becoming. Delusions of grandeur, I hear in my head, one of my mother's favorite phrases.

I don't remember when I went to see Gordon in his office. I was frustrated at the school, I told him. None of the directors had the talent of the brilliant young men I had served in college.

Where are the geniuses? I asked him.

What about you? he replied.

Imagine this: the school is still reeling from the two-week visit of the Living Theatre (founded 1947), a radical company just returned from tax exile in Europe, all dressed in black, and stoned, I would learn, on LSD. *The centre cannot hold*, we kept saying (W. B. Yeats, "The Second Coming," 1919). After Christmas, I take the trip to Mexico with Bob. Sometime after that I become pregnant by L or by the photographer. In March I do not get my period for a second time and get tested.

As I wake in the recovery room: No sexual relations or you'll get an infection, the doctor intones.

The day after the abortion, in L's apartment, we begin to make love. I tell L I have cramps but not about the abortion. He goes out to teach. Very bad cramps but also a little blood and the scrape feeling. Coat hanger: I damn near died, a friend told me about hers. I call the doctor. Did you have sexual relations? No. He'll call the drugstore, he says, prescribe. He thought I was lying. I thought I was lying. L had suddenly wanted me, and my body wanted him back. I pushed his hand away. I have an infection, I say, not the whole truth, and then he is so sympathetic, so nice—picking up the prescription, cuddling me into bed— that I tell him.

I had an abortion.

He began to shout: I would have married you! the line I remember. He leapt up, as if the bed had burned him.

Within my sobbing, the disinterest of rationality, from nowhere, self-interest: I could not marry him. His other girlfriends in New York, the shots—it's medical, he says, rubber cord wrapped around his arm, insists I inject him. Speed and vitamins: I'd stop the car at a medical office on Central Park South.

I remember the turn of L's body after the shouting, his exit from the small bedroom, how he put his jacket on and left the apartment.

O r this: I tell L I am pregnant. He romantically proposes, and I say yes. He has an idea, me doing the work of the kitchen, him the father. The panic of trying to survive as a working artist. I was a young woman with money, problem solved.

A wedding? My imagination sticks like a needle on an LP. Do I tell my parents and plan the ceremony? Modest, wearing a suit and high heels, a little veiled hat? As in real life, they have not met L, though my mother had investigated him through another New York writer who taught at the school. Was it in a small chapel, or did we go to a justice of the peace?

The scenario I invent is as opaque as a college reunion update. I live with him in his shabby Thirteenth Street one bedroom. No room for a baby. I rent another apartment, a livable one. Or do I buy one? I could have afforded the tree-lined street. My mother desperately helps me acquire furniture, appropriate linen and lamps, china and glassware. I'm seven months pregnant and the duplex is on Tenth Street between Fifth and Sixth—the now unattainable street—him mostly in New Haven, then in late summer off to Chicago. I'll join him there "after the baby is born."

Meeting a friend from college, I present myself in the best possible light, enumerating L's accomplishments. I always thought you'd have a big wedding, she says. After lunch, she puts me in a taxi and I go home. Somehow L is in New York two days a week, and he's gotten me to buy a piano— he and a director are working on lyrics for a production of his translation of *Rise and Fall of the City of Mahagonny*, so timely! In real life, they imagined Linda Ronstadt (b. 1946) the star, fierce soaring hit soprano; she's just my age. My imagination freezes, me in a corner watching and silent, the baby due in October.

Sweetie, my mother says on the phone, do you want the red glasses—we have thirty of each; you can have eight. Also I have Great-Granny's rug; it might work in your dining room. When she actually said those things a few years later,

I was holding the receiver to my ear, no almost-born child. Such a relief, my actual life.

I drive the shimmery blue Corvair forward. I worry about what's immediately in front of me, what I can see, but I do not concern myself with what's behind me. As for what's ahead, I do not imagine that I am picturing the future.

IV

I Didn't Walk Differently

How do they see inside you? The thing is always so cold. So, so cold and somehow a noise, a sliding metallic noise. If the doctor is nice, he or she says, This will be cold.

In a photograph from the 1970s I have always remembered, several women surround a woman lying on her back, feet in the metal stirrups, her knees bent and almost all the way open; the other women lean in to look through a speculum at her insides: an alien place. Sometime after the photo was taken, after seeing the movie *Jaws* (1975), a friend of mine said the shark didn't scare her: I'm not afraid of vagina dentata.

I've come from the chiropractor. It's my hip that she corrects and right after the appointment it hurts to walk. It didn't hurt like that after the abortion, even though something had been taken from inside me. I didn't walk differently.

I can't forget my first gynecological exam, the metal claw of the speculum opening me. I must have been in college. I search out the famous speculum photograph while choosing images for a book of feminist writing—no question that we will include it. A year later, I am selecting images for a book talk at an august Boston women's club: Not the photo of the pelvic exam, surely not that, says the organizer. In her tone, disgust and fear: Of course not. I assure her, as if women in the club had not all had those exams.

In a museum, I'm looking at a Jasper Johns drawing in a wood frame. Tiny pencil strokes increasingly closer to one another so that the surface moves from shades of gray almost to white. Embedded at the center is a small round shape of very bright light, a mirror. *Untitled*, 2007, says the label, *graphite pencil on paper, with objects*. Standing in front of it, I see myself reflected in the tiny circle of mirror in the midst of the complicated gray, and I take a photograph. When I get home, I scroll through the images on my smartphone and find it: in the mirror, a corner of my orange phone case and behind it, a piece of myself.

A winter weather advisory on my phone's screen when I wake up at 3:47 a.m. It's a teaching day and I'd gone to sleep at 9:30. My brother-in-law tells me that if he wakes up in the night, he thinks through the piece of music he is writing. It is hard for me to write on the day that I teach, but I am frightened not to since I am fighting loss of faith. When I tell a feminist archivist that I'm writing about my abortion, she says Fantastic! When I tell my Hollywood friend, she's silent, and then, Well, if you say so. When I was giving poetry readings with gangs of raucous women, she was working at *Saturday Night Live* with gangs of soon-to-be famous raucous men.

A mirror from the past—it's dirty and hard to clean.

Dirty because it's old? Or because it's been buried and I dig it up? I love it when I can dig things up and make them new again. Literally dig through old papers, or figuratively. I had the idea that if I looked into the small disk of mirror in the gray painting, I would see way back—behind the orange corner of my phone case, beyond the image of myself now. Not only pictures of me: take lower Seventh Avenue now, even the small makeup mirror I carry in my purse shines back the small theatre in the building that is now a restaurant called Boucherie. V and I walk up to the box office and get tickets for a play set in the lobby of a run-down hotel (*Hot*

L Baltimore, 1975). A woman my age, played by a woman I knew in college, enters "the lobby." Since then, when I'm in a restaurant or an airport, I see that everyone moving through public space is performing an act of self-presentation.

Or this: He was a playwright, his day job press agent for the professional theatre attached to the school, and he encouraged me to write something for the hip new journalism review starting up at the university. A great British actor was playing the lead in Pirandello's *Henry IV* (Kenneth Haigh, 1968), and I wrote something about a king on a horse in the streets of New Haven. The piece wasn't accepted—That doesn't matter, the press agent said, you're a writer. Which I took with a grain of salt, by which I mean I couldn't find a vein, a voice. Had I been my own student, I would have said, Try anything, write *yourself* as the king on the horse.

Come on over for a drink, he says on the phone. It is nighttime and it's the press agent. I put on new blue jeans and a navy cable-knit turtleneck sweater. His New Haven apartment was in an old-fashioned house up some avenue; it had wonderful high ceilings. We had a drink, and he asked if I would like to have an affair with him. I turned him down. That sounds confident, but really, I didn't understand how to put together what he looked like with how I thought about men. I was attracted to his mind. I should at least have kissed him. If I had, might I have been safer? Not fallen into the thrall of L? He had expressive hands and was funny and self-deprecating. Why not fall in love with the one who truly encourages you?

We'll give a dinner party for you, he said decades later. I was coming to Los Angeles to promote my first book. He and his wife, several old friends, all in our late fifties, all of us on a terrace overlooking the Hollywood Hills, like something from the 1940s. He was now a novelist and screenwriter and she was a feminist journalist I'd known in New York. I'm so proud of you, he said in his toast.

So arrogant, I think now, turning him down like that, not getting to know him. He actually saw me, but I didn't see him at all.

Through an Internet search, I find her in Texas, cold call her. She was one of my two close women friends at the school. Diana. Same voice and accent. She had white-blond hair and charm, small and wiry. She arrived my second year, an acting student, and we became friends. Did we meet when Dan fell for her? He had a romantic streak, a reddish scraggly beard, fresh from the 1968 demonstrations at Columbia; his best friend ended up in Attica, one of those police killings in the early 1980s. *Radical* was the word. By the spring of our second year, he and Bob had left the school, but Diana and I stayed, uneasy and restless. She was at our parties and maybe she came to the Berkshires on weekends—Dan and Bob were crashing there with our teacher Gordon, whose contract had not been renewed—teaching differences with the dean. We were all "writing novels." Just after he finished it a decade later, Bob's novel burned in a fire.

One day that February, Diana called me up. She was pregnant. At the time I assumed she was with Dan, but all these years later, she says no, the father was her boyfriend, a Texan at Yale Law School. When I say she called me about her pregnancy, I get a niggling memory that maybe Dan called first. In our way of thinking then, her getting pregnant was an unfortunate accident and I was the one with money, but now she tells me the law school boyfriend paid for it, but yes, she asked me to drive; I had the car. I remember that I hesitated—an abortion, a real fear we could be arrested. The place was in New Jersey, the time late at night, the outskirts of a town with rows of ranch houses, bungalows with steps up from the street.

I climbed the stairs with her, the streetlight illuminating her white-blond hair. We knocked on the door, which opened into the room where the abortion would take place. The doctor told me to go back outside and wait in the car. I remember the wait, the small ugly houses, and no one on the street. Did I go up to the door as she staggered out? That's what I wrote later, "She staggered out." Now it comes to me she was wearing a raincoat, a beige trench coat, and that I had to hold her up and help her into the car, the drive home at least two hours. I do not think she spent the night at my apartment. Why not? She called the next day or Dan did. She was in the hospital bleeding heavily—now, she says I damn near died. They gave her a D&C, effectively another abortion. It took her days to recover. She was why I didn't want to have an abortion at that place in New Jersey, her bleeding why I went to the kindly psychiatrist.

I hadn't seen her again, but I remember a call in the 1980s. You were in the entourage of a famous Nashville singer, right? Oh yes, oh that. Later, a novelist, an MFA in Houston, single mother to an adopted son. Yes, you drove me there, she says. Yes, tell my story.

Again, I wake in the night: 3:00 a.m., again a teaching day ahead—how to get back to sleep? Take a bath. Gagy, her real name Aägot. In the heat of the water she comes back, arms, open, large arms. She was Norwegian. A very nice lady, my mother wrote my father when she met her, pregnant with me and looking for a baby nurse. He's stationed on Guam, the end of the war. After that, no matter where we lived, Gagy came when a new baby was born. I have a snapshot on my bureau—she's about to sail for Norway, first trip back, all dressed up, a suit, a hat, corsage on her jacket. She's carrying what she always called "a pocketbook."

Gagy, I got pregnant and I had an abortion. I was all alone.

I might have said that, but I didn't. The phone rang and I picked it up, no way then to tell who was calling. She was already weeping, desolate that I had a "hippie boyfriend." She had raised her three children alone in the Woodlawn section of the Bronx in an eighth-floor walk-up with a midnight-blue carpet. I loved sitting around the kitchen table with her sister and grown-up daughter speaking Norwegian and eating a stinky cheese called Liederkranz.

Just marry Rob Fowler, she said through her tears; he was the other infant she cared for while she cared for me. Apparently, she had always dreamed we would marry. He and I kissed once when we were children, playing hide and seek in the dark, but I never knew him.

Sad woman who knows nothing about the new world we are making. Is it the young woman's cruelty that rouses the woman in her seventies from sleep to draw her own hot bath?

In a movie about abortion in 1969 (*Call Jane*, 2022), a young woman is talking to another young woman: It's a simple procedure. Like having a tooth pulled.

That summer I slept with (had sex, did not spend the night with) an actor who later won an Academy Award and the younger-than-me son of a famous writer of novels with Madison Avenue characters. At an opening night party, I met V, whom I'd live with later. He had lots of shiny dark brown hair and round horn-rimmed glasses; he talked a blue streak and lived with a woman named Joy, and no, he wouldn't kiss me, not even once.

Can we just have lunch?

Not while I'm living with Joy, he said, which gave me hope. Was that the night I wore a black crocheted minidress that showed a lot of my skin?

I don't know how sleeping with all those other men led to my visiting L in Chicago sometime in the fall. I had decided to leave drama school, shipped him my green sofa and all my Beatles records, believing that I would soon move to Chicago and live with him. When I began therapy in New York that fall, and the psychiatrist asked if I planned any "major life changes," I told him it was very possible I would soon marry.

I'm Zooming with rows of biographers, people I have seen on and off for thirty years, one of them, a friend since college. I last talked to her, both weeping, on the phone when a close friend of ours suddenly died. We all introduce ourselves by

subject—the Schuyler sisters, Keith Haring, W. E. B. Du
Bois. Surprising tightness in the chest when I mutter *memoir,*
abortion. Why does telling all these people I've had one make
me nervous? I've already written about it at least three times.
Life writing, I add, and exhale.

It's like cleaning out the basement, my first psychiatrist
said once as I reached for a cigarette. Are you going to dig
down or just leave it there? He advised leaving it undug.

Someone outside my window is drilling in stops and starts.

Were you alone? asks a new friend. I told only two people,
I say, and tell her about how they sent me flowers, the doctor
furious when he saw them beside my bed, berating me, red
faced, stomping out of the recovery room: I said not to tell.
Therapeutic abortion was effectively legal, but in practice it
was a loophole. He must have been terrified. A black-clad
SWAT team creeps into the room of beds, wrenches his arms
behind his back, jerks me from the recovery cot.

I spent two weeks in jail, I could have said to my
consciousness-raising group a year later, me chain smoking
in a circle of women my age, talking about our lives as women,
one subject at a time—sex, patriarchy, abortion: My father
kept it out of the newspapers, I'd tell them.

It's 1970, and I'm walking down the street with friends sometime after the Kent State killings—you can't believe it, four
unarmed students shot dead by the Ohio National Guard.
We pass a group of white men in hard hats outside an Irish
bar, of which there were still many in New York. They are
laughing and talking. They don't even look at us, young
women with long shiny hair. No, I say to myself, there will
be no revolution.

A son, I always thought, and some time ago, because
of how I imagine his eyes, I decided L was the father.
I don't remember the color of the photographer's eyes, and
I never saw him again, but when I ran into L at that party
in my forties, our son would have been in his twenties.
That was when L told me he had just been approached by a
grown-up daughter from a long-ago one-night stand—she
was a psychologist, he told me, somewhere in the Midwest.

Isn't that what children do, seek out missing parents?

If I'd had the son, would I have seen L again? Even
seen him at a party in my forties? Let's say my son was out
of college by then and in medical school—where in medical
school? Maybe in my alternative life, the reason I go teach
in Iowa is that my son is at medical school there.

I have him call me Mama because it makes me feel loved, not Mommy, which we called my mother, who would still have been alive when my son was born. If I'd had a child, would it have been more or less likely that I would have married? In my actual life, I was always looking for a great love—the kind that starts at a high temperature and calms over time, embers steady. What would I have looked for in a lover if I'd had a child?

My son and I go to our favorite restaurant and sit in a corner booth. I had never lied to him, but I sort of do now: We loved each other very much and then we broke up and didn't see each other again for a very long time.

Or I sit at the small table opposite my son and say, So, it's time for me to tell you about your birth, and then I tell him about myself as a young woman, about loving L and about my naive encounter with the photographer, including that I thought seeing myself nude in photographs might reassure me about my body. What is he supposed to do with that? I want him to understand I did not know how to take care of myself. He was sort of a friend and I wasn't attracted to him, I say; but before he took the photos, we drank scotch and I had my clothes off for the camera and we had sex that I didn't want.

I might be in tears by now, my son would hold my hands and tell me he loves me, bringing to mind the gentleness I have seen in my sisters' sons. I would tell him more about L, his talent, and about how I once met two of his uncles, British music hall comics with Cockney accents, at the New Yorker Hotel. What do you want to do? I'd ask him.

Are you sure he's my father?

Yes, because of your eyes, I say.

But do you really know? asks my son.

Do you want to do a DNA test, I ask.

And just like that, another scene to imagine: meeting L and asking if he will agree to a cheek swab. The thing is, I tell my son, when I told him about the abortion, he said he would have married me, but I didn't think he loved me. It's all pouring out of me. There was so much he didn't mean that in the end I realized I couldn't put myself or you in his hands. Here my imagination jams, like a car that won't start when you turn the key.

L was sleepy looking when I saw him again, as if stopping occasional heroin and the speed and vitamin concoction had killed off his life force. By then I had published books of poems and memoir. He was overweight, no longer dressed in Italian cashmere turtlenecks, no longer those narrow hips. He wanted to make love—anything you want, sweetheart—and though for some reason I wanted to comfort him, I couldn't do it. The man I had so desired, who might have impregnated me, was barely a figment. He was living in the Chelsea Hotel again, his rent underwritten by his old friend, the famous painter who supported him for decades.

Why not stage it there, the DNA request that occurs in my imagination? El Quijote is still there, but for this occasion, I imagine it as it was during the era before restaurants became polished and shiny, before so many walls were glass. L took me to those dark, cozy restaurants and later V took me, initiation into a world where you learned how to read a Spanish menu, then an Italian one, then, oh, let's go to a Korean restaurant. The saddest thing about L losing his looks was the loss of the curl in his hair. It's almost seven o'clock when I arrive—I am always on time, but L, I remember, is often late. I take a seat and order sparkling water. I wait there with my Pellegrino. I am still living in the imagined apartment I bought on Tenth Street, a big apartment for my son and me, which I could have afforded then.

Old man L. He's wearing khaki and has quite a belly. He sits down opposite me and says, How are you, my love, brushing fingers down my cheek. Which makes me a bit sick to my stomach. Does he actually say My love or was it Baby, or Pussy, the endearment I hated.

My son wants to know his father, I say. Have I ever told L about the photographer? I tell him now, without going into specifics: You remember how it was then . . . Did L then tell me he too had been unfaithful?

Well, I did sleep with Carol a few more times, I have him admit.

We'd like you to take a DNA test, just to be sure you're the father.

If that's what you want, he says, and then the waiter comes and we order paella.

You come right up against a thing and you can't figure out what to do, how to work it out. Not a thing that presents as a clear choice, rather a knot from which there are so many exits, there is none. This is so unlike those situations in which you fly, ideas firing, pop, pop, pop, and your language opens into a spangled firework over the ocean. I want to write about not being wanted, but nothing comes. I think back over my unrealized loves, how each time it seemed to my imagination that he, or she, later again he, would solve it. Solve what? The problem of who I am. I'd bother the question, stick with a lover for years, once for a decade because of one memorable night, until I am worn out by wanting. The sentence that comes to me is *It got too sad.*

Get a Corvair, my handsomest cousin said, and he'd have it worked on by a racecar driver named Don Yenko (1927–87): more horsepower, dual straight pipe exhaust and a spoiler on the trunk. A Yenko Stinger, Stage One. The car arrived the spring of my senior year in Cambridge—bright cerulean blue with a tinge of purple in certain light. I remember the two-hour drives from New Haven to New York—I roar down I-95 and make my way into town on the Major Deegan.

Once, driving back to New Haven, I get stopped by the police and have to pull out the special letter from Don Yenko testifying that the straight pipe exhaust is original equipment, otherwise there would be an enormous fine. Another time, I was stopped for speeding and taken into a police station, had to call someone to come get me. I loved to drive and listen to the radio. I remember it being dark and cold and I'd be driving fast and trailer trucks would start to follow me, two of them close me in, keep up with me if I speed up, so I feel crammed in, that they will mash me between them. My heart pounds when I realize they're doing this on purpose, young woman who craves quick acceleration.

What I want to get at is the notion of a woman in her early twenties, twenty-one, twenty-two, driving in her souped-up Corvair. Souped up implies inelegant and the car was elegant. I remember being in that car the summer after college with

Paul Schmidt, older, *queer*—he used that word even then and was the handsomest man I had ever seen—Vuitton luggage, which you could buy then only in Paris, fluent in Russian and French. It was just the two of us, him at the wheel, driving 120 miles an hour at sunrise, back to Cambridge from a party in Manchester-by-the-Sea.

V

The Beauty of Rust

Tanglewood, her tangled hair. Lawns and picnics. Beethoven, Schubert, and Dvořák, sometimes Leonard Bernstein (1918–90), but this summer, rock 'n' roll in the temple of the classical and the scent of marijuana. I sit inside, though not that close. Tiny on the stage in shades of orange tie dye and she looks ravaged, my shredded insides singing, *Another little piece of my heart.* She was a young white woman from Texas. I had thought of her as having a body like mine, curvy not angular, but she was skinny. She threw an arm up and dropped it and the music came to a halt—very loud and then complete silence. *Another little piece of my heart now, baby.* Take and devour, right on key but close to a scream, on the stage, orange, red, including her long hair. "Ball and Chain" and we stand and cheer. There's a photograph of her on an

album cover, a hat, a big smile, vintage velvet and pearls.
Like a flame across the dark stage—an arsonist setting fire
to herself. Dead in a year, a few weeks before I turn twenty-five (Janis Joplin, 1943–70).

Why did I get into a shouting match with the doorman whose
name was Whitey? New Haven, 1969. What I remember is
screaming at him, him looking at me in horror, me separate
from the self standing there screaming at him. What had
happened? Was I drunk? I think I was often drunk, that once
in a while I puked, the bathroom in front of me as I head to
my bedroom to the right and Gami's brass bed.

When I was admitted to the school to learn how better to
produce plays and publicize them, I knew I was lying. I didn't
know I was betraying myself.

I didn't have a self, and I had not found a way to say that.

I didn't have a voice either, as in my chest something
seized and I couldn't speak. I couldn't finish a sentence. Miss
Klaiber, at the blackboard—a straight line, diagonals separate subject, verb, object; clauses hang off the line. I love the
intricacies, the twiglike prepositional phrases. I leave out the
subject: the arty sentence fragment. And the object: can't
think it through. With a self, I could have thought it through.

Didn't I know I was irreplaceable?

The beauty of that dark-rust color on blazing white. Honor
has become "a woman" my mother wrote to a friend. I had
triumphed over something—what next? At first I didn't
attach it to childbirth, I don't think, or to fertility. I didn't
know the word *fertility* except that my grandmother dug in
her rose garden and explained the earth was fertile.

Sanitary napkins were like small white beds with tails on
either end. You had a "belt" that was elastic with a flat metal
hook on either end that might cut into you. Through those
hooks you snagged the tails of the sanitary napkin. Why was
it called a napkin when it was a thick ungainly pad? One was
always afraid of leaking, revelation to others that you were
bleeding. It was a game of chicken: how to know when to
change it so you wouldn't turn red. Is that why my mother
called it the curse? And then the cramps, which deformed
you, the heaviest feeling of ache at the base of your abdomen,
caused by an imbalance of hormones, it was said.

The curse. Why a curse? Its arrival meant you were not
pregnant, a reprieve. As I became interested in making a
distinction between my femaleness and the maleness of
men, I began to think of menstruation as a power that
connected me to the life of my body. The vibration of pain,
no matter how extreme, made the shape of my womb actual,

and the drench of blood purged and purified, all poisons carried away.

Your abortion was a choice you made, he says.

Not really, I reply and explain that the word *choice* replaced *pro abortion* nearly a decade after I made my decision.

But you did make a choice. . . Robert, who was born in the 1980s, is insistent on this point.

Okay, I say, but I think of making a choice as something thought out and considered, which my abortion was not.

You knew what you wanted to do with your life.

No, I did not know what I wanted to do.

You wanted to be a writer.

Possibly, but the idea was so remote that I couldn't verbalize it, not even to myself.

Remote—a distant filmy image. Even when I moved to New York in 1969 and told everyone I was going to write "a novel," the intention seemed to hover outside my body. I had never heard of *A Room of One's Own* (1929), let alone read Virginia Woolf. Dropped from memory was the college class in which the instructor, a novelist, a young man, declared my story the best of the semester, and Sunday mornings with the graduate student, not a boyfriend, to whom I read my first poems.

You were in the forefront.

The forefront of what?

Of feminism, he says. You were one of the first.

Not one of the very first, and there was barely any feminism when I had my abortion. No abortion rights movement.

But the Miss America protest . . .

I read about it in the *New York Times*, but it felt like a stunt, like something the Yippies would do. A stunt. (Youth International Party, founded 1967)

What about *The Feminine Mystique*? (Betty Friedan, 1963)

My mother read that, not me until much later. I had no consciousness that such a thing done by women could be serious. I had never heard of feminism.

Finally he has no reply.

What I had faintly heard of was women's liberation, and when I got to New York I went looking for it. I met a woman accused of conspiracy to bomb. I confused what she was doing with women's liberation, which I had read about in the *Village Voice* (weekly, 1955–2017). If I weren't involved in this, she said, meaning the court case about her bombing, I would look for the feminists. When I heard the words "the feminists," I got a chill. Glimmer of a self. Later I would say feminism allowed me to place myself at the center of my own narrative, by which I meant my own existence. At the time, I had no language for that idea.

I was in search of it, I tell Robert, but in secret.

Why in secret?

I was still with L, I say. He was so angry by then, speeded up, hitched to be the most radical, which was why I went to a speech by a Black lawyer named Flo Kennedy. She was a feminist—If men could get pregnant, abortion would be a sacrament—but at the time she was representing Black Panthers. I thought you were a pig, she told me later to explain her vague reply when I asked where I could find Panther defense.

S ure, he'd come to see me in the Berkshires, he said on the phone. I told the producer how much I admired L and of course she'd heard of him. He arrived and I took him to the big gray house I'd rented where I lived with a friend from the school, his rock band, and Dan, still writing his novel. My room was enormous and on a single shelf on the wall above my bed, I lined up all the books I thought would remind L how much he loved me—the Little Red Book by Chairman Mao (1964), *Soul on Ice* by Eldridge Cleaver (1968), *Revolution for the Hell of It* by Abbie Hoffman (1968). Not a single volume by a woman. It was the summer of Woodstock and the first landing on the moon, and L was on his way to Chicago to make a new theatre with an old friend.

I didn't want L to have anything to do with my writing, a secret—even now, I can retrieve his voice: no good, no good. All I remember about him in my bedroom was his chuckle as he complimented me on the political perfection of the row of books on that small shelf.

By mid-September, I was in New York, settled at the Chelsea Hotel, a room with a double bed, a shabby dark-blue carpet, a french door opening onto a balcony, a stained-glass lunette—vine of bright green, flowers royal blue, turquoise, magenta. I set up a table and chair to face the window, for the first time positioning my writing desk the way I have all my life since. Who knows what I wrote. I have a lot of my early writing but not the beginning of my novel, if indeed I started one.

Had we actually broken up? Or was it just that he hadn't called and I had decided, finally, to think of us as broken up? There were days of solitude in the company of my fledgling self, a typewriter in front of me, balcony overlooking the street, colors through the half-moon window, open sky. I was on the third floor, I think, but I took the elevator nonetheless. I remember brass plaques to dead writers, all of them men, at the entrance of the hotel. People like Leonard Cohen, Viva, Janis Joplin, Andy Warhol, and Bob Dylan frequented the Chelsea that fall. I may have shared the elevator with any one of them.

And then one day the phone rang and it was L, suddenly in New York. He asked me to go out to dinner, burgers at his friend Bradley Cunningham's new jazz club on University Place. I'm at the Chelsea, he'd say on the telephone to this friend or that. He didn't mention me. Another night we went to Casey's, a French restaurant run by a Chinese drug dealer that had great food, and afterward again to Bradley's. Were we living together now? We went to Bradley's almost every night. Paul Desmond. Elvin Jones. Maybe Dexter Gordon, even John Coltrane. I knew nothing of jazz. Always L's friends, Bradley with his girlfriend my age, and a beautiful woman always on her own, a writer with prematurely white hair. She wore gauzy lavender and spoke as if nothing mattered. I wanted to matter.

Leave him, says you, the reader, exasperated. But I have nowhere to go. No friends yet, no job, only the psychiatrist my pain took me to. Like honey you can't be free of unless you lick it off. Like the muck on a mousetrap that will not let go.

My imagination was overcompetent. I'd picture us, artist adventurers in revolutionary Chicago, he and his friends; the theatre they'd started called the Body Politic—transformation was the word for what they did: as in Ovid, in an instant, human to animal. I'd write while he was at rehearsal.

This was before the discourse of *unavailable*. Exploitative, the psychiatrist said; he's a sociopath. What did anyone else know about the gleaming center of my heart? I started writing poems, but he was in my way. I was certain that beneath his cruelty, he really loved me.

An angle of light on his face, my ten-years-older friend says of falling in love with her husband.

Leave him, repeats the reader, who would have left him pages ago. At fifty, I was still falling in love like that: he's at the phone, calls me up, he's driving now, thinking of me, if this happens and that, he will call, we will meet, we will make love, he'll remember he's in love with me. You're asking him to have a conversion experience, a friend says kindly.

Deep in my files, I discover a poem I wrote in 1970: "Hate Letters." "The ghosts of my / involvement with you / stain my retinas." And another: "It hurts like some great / broken bottle / shredding me inside."

The year is 2022, and I imagine this: A woman and her friend drive to an abortion clinic across the border in Mexico. A police car screeching. Gangs of men track you down. Flash of the recovery room in New Haven. Next thing you know, they'll round up women like me who had abortions in 1969,

no statute of limitations; they drag me in, based on what
I disclose here, not only my own abortion but the one I drove
my friend to in New Jersey, the ones two friends from college
had, the legal one I encouraged _____ to have in 1975. I don't
know if Diana from Texas is exempt, or _____ because she
had children later.

A woman who publishes a book about her long-ago
abortion is imprisoned when she gives a public reading at
a bookstore in Texas where she once read her poems. You
think they're lining up for you, but they crowd in, and pour
accelerant on your stack of books and light a match.

I was afraid that morning in New Haven. Not of the police
but of not being allowed to have the operation.

In an elegant apartment in the Dakota, a Sunday night kitchen
supper. What year was yours? asks my friend. 1969, I say.

Mine too, she says, what month?

April, I answer.

June, she says. Hers was in Mexico, and they were in
love; he too said he'd marry her. They were using a condom.
She had been accepted into a graduate program, the first
woman to study with a famous historian. Why would I get
married and have the baby? she says, exasperated. I had my
whole life in front of me. A long career in public service,

reproductive rights, also marriage and two children. The husband, also at the table, is a lawyer and as versed in reproductive rights as she is.

Certain details are incomprehensible to young women. They look at me, blankly, as I try to explain that the source of orgasm was once a matter of debate—vagina or clitoris?—the clitoris known to exist, but just barely. William H. Masters and Virginia E. Johnson (*Human Sexual Response*, 1966) were the equivalent of pre-Columbian mapmakers—the accuracy of their discoveries becoming more precise with time. A psychiatrist named Mary Jane Sherfey (1918–83), sweet looking and white haired when I heard her speak in the 1970s, was the Columbus of the clitoris, but an activist named Anne Koedt liberated the terrain when she published a pamphlet titled *The Myth of the Vaginal Orgasm* (1968).

We are standing on Thirteenth Street in Manhattan when my sister tells me she tries to have two orgasms a day.

The sofa has gone soft and the seat is a bit low so it is an effort to get up. I work to stay in shape, but cardio has always been difficult. Loneliness, I think, and also some sort of injury at birth, so that running, walking fast, or riding a bicycle can jam up my right side and give me a migraine. This morning I am considering how to present myself at this age, when the body's future has been foreclosed, as in, *I will never become a runner, I will never become a yoga instructor, Will I ever have sex again?*

My father, when we're in therapy together in my fifties, explains about his marriage to my mother: We were not a good sexual fit. Too much information, we say now. At lunch at a restaurant in Washington years after my abortion my mother and I have a sad conversation about her first orgasm; she was in her forties: What's the matter, Jenny? my father exclaimed. I remembered introducing her to the philosopher. I was certain she knew what happened to me in bed with him when she said, I wouldn't want to have an affair with him. She was older than forty by then and therefore orgasmic. I didn't want to repeat the story, but here it is again.

A young woman tells me that the bleeding frightens her, and I think of the beauty of rust on a white pad, even on new white underpants. I felt purified, I say, dark blood pouring out of me, how even the terrible pain of cramps seemed a sacred rite. It's 2012, and I was trying to understand why she had asked me to call her *they*, why she did not wish to remain a woman. I don't have language for it, they replied. Ah, I said. I understand. I told them that the bleeding was nothing to fear and that I hoped they would forgive me if

I seemed aggressive in offering my experience. Now, though, I ask myself why they would want to enter my history when they are so hard at work creating their own.

VI

I Do Need to Swivel My Body

A kind of gold light, you step into the room and all the faces turn toward you. Other students, actors from the company who will later become movie stars, a playwright who's had a culture-altering hit: you walk toward them, a glass of wine suddenly in your hand. We all smoke, me marijuana for the first time, cigarettes absent from memory, even the smell. The movie-star-to-be and the culture-altering playwright had once joined me on the street outside the theatre, inexplicable since I did not know them. The playwright scrutinized me, Eyes far apart, he said; I like that, said the movie-star-to-be. And there he is now across the room, and he looks at me, eyes glittering, turns away this time, as if I belong on another channel.

Where is L?

This was at the end of the first year, and I had not met him. There's the soon-to-be-world-famous British playwright. I don't know Bob and Daniel yet, oh and there's the one female doctoral student in criticism talking to the one woman playwright in their class. The dean looks different with a drink in his hand, and Gordon is characteristically getting delightfully tipsy. I haven't forgotten the day he challenged me to be a genius—*What about you?* Ever since then I have been trying to write, sit down at my blue desk and work on the play, the protagonist a quadriplegic professor in a wheelchair—nothing I've written so far bears showing to anyone, but I have the genius question tucked away. Praise is a form of scrutiny, a friend would say years later. I didn't yet understand genius as I understand it now—the ability to bring forth in ideal form absolutely everything within your imagination.

I pull another cigarette from my purse and the music is Ella Fitzgerald (1917–96), which makes me think of my mother and feel safe. Such conversation, what's on that one must see and what book everyone has just read. Maybe Susan Sontag (1933–2004) is at the party, but I don't yet know who she is. Gay men, then quasi-closeted, openly flirting. The smell of scotch, whiff of marijuana. I stand all evening, high heels, I'm sure, and a slightly sexy dress. I remember it as my second glamorous New York party (the first the summer after college, the book on everyone's lips *Making It* (1967), by someone named Norman Podhoretz, the quintessential New York intellectual, I was told). After this party, after this night, phone numbers apparently exchanged, I'll have a date with the glittery-eyed actor who became a movie star but once played a notable Hamm in *Endgame*.

But that party was a year and a half earlier. Now Gordon and his partner—we didn't use that word then—are teaching in Chicago, where L was then also teaching. Also dropped out of the drama school and teaching there were Everett, a director with dark-brown shiny hair and a bowl cut, and his wife, Gwen, a designer.

Come for tea, Gordon said, or a drink.

Daylight as I walk again into the Upper West Side building near Central Park, take the elevator. Daylight so the room is not the golden sphere of the cocktail party. Carpets, I notice now, and so many books, carpets that suck up the sound as you walk. They were all in the living room at the back of the apartment. Everett always made me feel ill at ease. Once in Chicago, when I was visiting L, Everett and I were on a bus, and out the window on a shop sign, the word *warlock* flashed by. That's it, I thought, he's a warlock. He was always very kind so I don't know why I thought that. Now he and Gwen and Gordon and his partner are all in

New York for a few days, and we are sitting in the back of the apartment. Of course I want news of L but I do not ask for it, and then, suddenly, Everett, in his smooth voice, is telling me that the previous week, L had married a woman named Nicole.

I'm thinking of scenes on crime TV when detectives sneak into an apartment to look for evidence when the person isn't home. They pick the lock and go in, Glock held with both hands, arms outstretched, swiveling their bodies. Someone shouts Clear!, meaning no perpetrator, no danger. I don't think I need to enter with a gun drawn, but I do need to swivel my body, look to the right and then to the left in one expert motion. Boss, there's something here, is what the detective says if the show is British, corpse coming into view, blood up the wall of a ransacked room.

Who is Nicole? I ask. When I published the book in which I first wrote about L, I got a Facebook message from a woman named Nicole. Since there were three Nicoles in a class I taught once, the name at first didn't flash. As if I hadn't known, she indicated she had once been married to L and that she would be happy to tell me about him if I liked. I thought the offer extremely odd, as if I hadn't learned him by heart. Yes, sure, I posted back, but I never heard from her again.

Did all of them know about L and Nicole, even when I'd gone on and on about moving to Chicago? Had they all been to the wedding? Nicole in a hippie dress and L touching her cheek instead of mine. Having the kind of sex with her that he wanted to have with me when I visited that fall, which I'm not going to describe because it disgusts me. I was twenty-four years old and I went along with it. I was looking for a life. The self at the typewriter, where is she? I am in a Chicago bed I hardly remember, alone and weeping, and at least one night, he doesn't come back at all.

L was now married to a woman named Nicole and I am sitting in daylight in a night apartment as if at the center of a big circle closing in until I disappear, to reappear at a burger joint across the street having dinner with two young men to whom I tell nothing. Who is Nicole? I don't know where the details come from, but I learn that she also has long brown hair and is about my age. Nor do I know how they met and I never learned.

I don't ask if they were all at the wedding in some city hall room in Chicago, smiles, kisses, squeezing of hands. Certainly L's lifetime friends, a director and his wife who had many daughters, celebrated with him. My acupuncturist, who is in the process of divorcing, just reminded me that marriage is not a contract between you and your beloved but between you and the state. The revolutionary L had entered into a contract with the state that linked him to a woman named Nicole who, like me, had long dark brown hair.

Come over and we'll have a drink then all go out to dinner, Gordon said on the phone, knowing it had fallen to him or Everett to do the decent thing, break it to me that L had married Nicole in a civil ceremony in Chicago.

The reader asks, why are you still "in love with" such a man?

In a BBC television series called *MI-5* (2002–11), a team of spies takes their seats around a table sometime early in the twenty-first century. Who gave the order? Who is the target? What is the identity of the person they call the subject?

I am the subject, but that does not mean I have a self.

You don't help enough, L kept complaining. When I think about what it meant for such a young woman to be sexually involved with a much older man, I consider the experience of becoming aroused by a sexual act completely new to you. I mean an act not prepared for or mutually discovered: the resulting orgasm takes you by surprise, and someone else claims what belongs to you, turning you over on a mattress on the floor, your red Mexican dress above your head, and somehow it doesn't hurt. You have become so great sexually, he says. It was as if I'd put more money on the table than I had.

I do need to swivel my body. What I mean is, swivel my self.

I remember a walk in Chicago with the wife of L's best friend, the one with several daughters, including the baby girl she's pushing in a stroller—we're talking about L and me. You should stop the pill and get knocked up, she said, then he'll marry you. *Get knocked up.* I hadn't told her about the abortion.

Y ou get right up here, she said.
    She was a nurse, activist, pregnant with the child of George, who had been arrested in a sweep of Black Panthers and was in jail. Had grown up in a small town in New Jersey, close to Camden. She was the strongest woman I knew. In her thirties, I imagined, but finding her obituary, I learn she was my mother's exact age, dying at ninety-nine in 2022. I was not able to fathom what must have been her terror, as at the time, a spark of celebrity surrounded her situation. Lily Farmer, my first older woman friend, the first Black woman I knew who dressed in traditional African fabric, wrapped and tied her head in a gele. Black Arts movement poets at the university. Nationalism was new and new to me.
    George had been indicted on conspiracy to murder a suspected government informant named Alex Rackley (1949–69), in the wake of a speech by Black Panther national

chairman Bobby Seale (b. 1936). I had helped organize this appearance with my friend Pam—a benefit for the new Black theatre she and George, also an actor, cofounded. I called the radical university chaplain, a friend of my father, mentor to my brother. Yes, certainly, Bobby Seale could speak in the chapel.

Old newspaper and magazine accounts, undertow of dread and J. Edgar Hoover informers, you never knew who. Rackley was not an informer, but no one knew it then; he was tortured and murdered by the Panthers; George had no part in the killing. Nor did I know then that George had been held in the basement with Rackley and would have been murdered but for a last-minute warning from the man said to have pulled the trigger of the gun that killed Rackley. A few years later, the charges against George would be dropped.

The arraignment in a bright New Haven courtroom is where Pam introduced me to Lily. We became friends; I would help her, money for the obstetrician, baby clothes—I had so much, and she was just scraping by. I'm often at her apartment for supper, once to watch the Supremes on *Ed Sullivan* (December 21, 1969).

In tears, I call and tell her about L's marriage. You get right up here, she says.

I drive to New Haven. Lily had found a bar with an open mic and signs me up. When I get to the apartment, she tells me I'm reading my poems that night. She would hear nothing of my resistance.

Something blue in an image and hidden rage. I step up to do my first reading ever. Through speakers set for jazz, comes my unrecognizable voice.

The manila folder appears now like a hat trick, in thick blue Sharpie, HM 1st Coll, inside, a faint xerox of typewritten pages: *Forty-Six Poems*, the earliest January 1969, so the dates match up. Actual poems, not the scribbles I remembered: "Your marriage hit / Me like a wet dishcloth / Across the eyes." And: "You're in contempt of my life."

Clapping after, and I almost stumble back to the table, Lily's unstoppable smile, and then Pam hugging me, also the girl from Levittown, and other friends Lily invited from the school.

I do not imagine that in my future life I will do this hundreds of times.

I'm going to write and tell him about the great poems you're writing, Lily says, with a conspiratorial smile. She knew L, and she had his number—he'd pay attention because she was Black. He doesn't know what he's let go of.

I didn't quite believe her, but she spoke with the authority of a woman with a self.

I dream the committee in charge of my future decrees that . . . Why can't I remember the rest, just minutes after I wake up?

The scene was so clear. I stood on the path then began to walk. Let's say a camera-bearing drone caught the view all the way from heaven. L is radiant, in his young body, and because he has died, I can now tell him what I hated about how he talked to me: No, you can't insult my writing, dismiss me because of the color of my skin, or the family I came from.

Sometime in the 1970s, I stand in a circle with a women's theatre group, I am Honor, daughter of Jenny, granddaughter of Fanny and Margarett, "who went mad and stopped finishing her paintings at thirty-five," as I put it in a poem I called "Polemic #1." I am a woman giving birth to myself, each of us declares, after recounting our "matrilineage."

Why, asks my friend, is the child in your imagination a son and not a daughter?

My mother, slapping me hard—only three times, but I remember each. Was I in the way of her set-aside self? Only three, but that was enough. I was afraid I would slap a daughter.

An antidepressant had become too expensive, the generic did not work, and a new drug made me feel uneasy. What had turned me, a great sleeper, into a fitful one? Overwork? My psychopharmacologist, a woman, switched me to a new drug and my sleep improved. She asked me to track irritability—out of the blue, I had snapped at two friends. The doctor and I identified a feeling—pain right up next to sensitivity. She surmised the pain came in part from repeated rejection, a natural way for a child to interpret the birth of a sibling. I tell her that my best writing often begins in that anger.

Two later lovers come into view, one a woman—we did nothing but have sex for days, and talked obsessively about our writing, about Virginia Woolf. The other was slip-on-the-ice who said, The first thing I'd do is knock you up. Lovemaking with him brought images of me with a pregnant body, and, for the first and only time, a desire to have a child. Finally, I marveled to friends, I understand what makes the world go round. But we used birth control and I didn't get pregnant and he went back to his wife.

A daughter would have had dark hair, would have looked like my mother, and would have had my mother's complexity. The son lolls in a meadow. I think I would have given him freedom and I think he would have sympathy. The girl, sallow like my mother when she was unhappy, will not even look at me.

A friend just made me a decoupage, a box covered with clips of images from my life. She kept asking questions like What is your favorite kind of dog and Is there a place you've seen you would call heaven. My favorite band and my favorite writers. Classical music, I said. Virginia Woolf. What dog? Dalmatians. Heaven was a park in the country of Georgia with trees centuries old and very green grass. A photograph of me as an infant with my mother and father who are so young they look like children. My mother just the age I was when I had my abortion and had not yet given up the misbegotten dream of first love. Another writer, James Baldwin, and you must include my dear friends Arthur and Inge—in a photo from an Argentine magazine, playwright and photographer whom I met when I was forty (Arthur Miller, 1915–2005; Inge Morath, 1923–2002): We thought you seemed a little lost. Nothing on the box marks the time of the abortion, which I now realize was when I began to surrender the primacy of real life and write.

It would be decades before I realized how hard I worked to find evidence of connection in a lover's voice, to conjure living together, a touch to my cheek. So much imaginative diligence squandered, I suddenly understood. Put it in your poems.

Last night in a dream, my mother is dying again and someone has stolen the blue flowering plant I sent her.

What I remember is the house in Washington and me walking into the bedroom. A month afterward? She is sitting in a large armchair, which faces the door. Their king-size bed is to my right with the arch of baby photos above the headboard, all nine of us as infants. I'm thinking that my brother Paul is there. My father certainly is.

I had an abortion, I said. I had not sat down and had not planned to say this. I remember my mother spoke first, a catch in the throat: When?

I think they asked who had gotten me pregnant and I said L, whom they knew had broken up with me.

A back-alley abortion?

No, in a hospital.

It's not exactly indifference that I remember, just that I was being blasé, invested in being blasé and sophisticated.

I wonder now what it would have been like if I'd told them when I found out I was pregnant. Where I then would have had the abortion. Or would I have been shipped off to one of those places where you give birth and put the child up for adoption?

The stage is bare except for the easy chair. The mother, in her midforties, sits there, the father hovers, the daughter, who is downstage, crosses up left. We hear the conversation as laughs and remarks, no identifiable words, and then the young woman's voice, I had an abortion. As I remember, my announcement bubbled up in the conversation. Had they been talking about some other young woman getting pregnant?

An overused device, I know, but I think it works: blackout.

An upperclassman wants to direct the Jean Giraudox play *A Duel of Angels* (1953). Why not? Gorgeous costumes.

The meeting was in the big lounge on the second floor of the drama center. We sat in a circle in modernist chairs. The brilliant young man who drank rum and Coke and never stopped smoking put forward the idea. There had never been a woman, but I could be president—though without artistic authority. I could not imagine objecting, so I comply, collude. I have convinced everyone including myself that producing is my sole ambition. A useful disguise for lack of confidence, a deft cover for anger. That's a little harsh—but operatively true.

From far away in her future, someone tells the young woman to protest, but she pays no attention.

I read the same books and took the same classes. I had the same conversations. I had ideas. I had learned to look at something on a stage and think about it, hour after hour of rehearsal: No, take a deep cross down right. Yes, raise that spot, we need to see her face. Can you say that as if you're hiding your sadness?

I knew how to look at something, watch it move through time and refine what I thought. I did not doubt that I was entitled to be on the earth, but in my mind the assertion was muddled.

At an opening that spring, I wear a silk shift with a diagonal that made it half red and half a stylish black geometric shape.

I kept buying clothes to cover it up—body, doubt, shame. Self? When a man reached beneath my clothes, I thought he was willing to encounter me. Is that what my friend meant when she said she slept with men for the conversations after sex?

At the reception after a memorial, I tell a man I know a story a mutual friend once told about him. They enter a party together—she is older and not his date but a coworker. Just watch, he tells her, and crosses the room, stands against a wall and smiles. *Just watch*. In a flash he's surrounded by women. He listens as I tell him the story and then, with a faint smile, he says, I am so glad that's over. It was exhausting.

VII

Mama Why

The oldest of my five younger sisters, her first child in the crook of her elbow: I always wanted to be a mother, she says.

Which shocked me—I mean confounded me, the idea of *wanting* to be a mother. And then, variously, each sister declares she wants a family, children, one even seeking out a husband who she believes will be a "good dad."

There is a way I can speak that is stentorian, and when I do, I am not present: I never wanted to be a mother. Distinct from: I didn't want a child.

I did not understand what it felt like to want a child.

I did not grieve the loss of my pregnancy, but I did grieve the loss of a younger self who had not yet made a

momentous decision on her own behalf. A termination. A loss
of innocence?

Your mother had you at twenty-two and you were older
than that.

I didn't feel ready, it was a shock.

A shock?

Getting pregnant was a shock.

Why weren't you more careful?

You can be careful and a mistake can happen. (I don't
want to admit I wasn't careful.)

A mistake?

Forget to take your pill or a hole in the condom or the
diaphragm slips.

All that equipment to not be a mother . . .

Not be a mother yet.

So there was a time when you wanted to be one?

To be a mother was what a girl wanted then, and I did
not. Once, years later, when I stroked a baby's skin and leaned
in to smell, I wanted a child, but the physical desire entered
my body only once—with the man I met when I slipped on
the ice. Soon, friends started to have babies, and my sisters.
By the time I was in my forties, I had learned to say, What
a beautiful baby! By my sixties I meant it.

Once when I was making love with another woman . . .

You had lovers who were women?

Yes, for more than a decade. Anyway, once when I was making love with another woman, she touched me between my legs, and suddenly, as if my mother were touching me there, I was an infant.

After the abortion, I returned to the theatre in the Berkshires for a second summer.

The first summer, I was thrilled just to get an interview; in preparation, I asked a New York director who taught at the school about the producer. She's a dyke who's had a bad season, he said, which scared me, as it was meant to. I was apprehensive as I entered the elevator to her office above the Palace Theatre on Broadway, the waiting room out of a scene from a Rosalind Russell movie (*His Girl Friday*, 1940).

The producer was a woman my mother's age with a round face and gray hair cut to her chin; listening, she had the sharp attentiveness of a bird, moving her head in little adjustments as you see birds do through binoculars. I liked her. She asked me to call her on my way back to New Haven. I stopped at a phone booth on the Merritt Parkway: I'll hire you, she said. Make me proud.

Pictures and features on the front page of the Arts and Leisure section of the *New York Times*, headlines in the

Berkshire Eagle—I did what I'd learned in publicity class. In November, after that first summer, the producer took me out for a drink at the King Cole Bar at the St. Regis, martinis and the Maxfield Parrish mural. The board had threatened to fire her because I overspent on ads by thousands of dollars. She found a way to pay off the debt and talked them into rehiring me. Make me proud, she said again. No one had told me there was a budget or how much it was, and no one was paying attention. I was so ashamed.

It's May, just weeks after the abortion, layout for the theatre brochure is due, and I am afraid of the budget constraints. I hire a friend from the design school instead of the glitzy New York designer; the brochure will have text rather than photographs, cheaper to print. Yellow with red letters. The season is complicated, I say, explaining my idea to the producer. The plays require thought: one is by Eugène Ionesco (1909–94), who will visit from Paris—how to frame a three-act called *Hunger and Thirst* as summer entertainment.

That term, I had been taking a writing class. The dean, when he visits the class, is startled by my presence, the only female in the room and not a writing student: What are you doing here?

My first essay was an account of Aretha Franklin (1942–2018) at the New Haven Arena—concert as theatre: *You make me feel like a natural woman*; just three years older than me, she compels an orchestra, holds an audience of four thousand. When I search for information about that concert, a ticket flashes on my phone's screen. Flesh pink, January 31, 1969. In just under three months, I'd have the abortion.

Three months later, a group photograph taken on a porch, the young woman at the center wears a checked minidress, legs crossed, hair pulled back, radiant smile, her housemates around her, Daniel, Jan and his rock band, long haired, in the custom of that summer of moon shot and Woodstock. Enough room in the big gray house, twenty minutes from the theatre, with a barn where the band wrote and rehearsed in the spirit of *Music from Big Pink* (the Band, 1968).

All summer, the young woman drove the blue Corvair up the valley to work and when she came home she cooked, secluded herself in her bedroom, read, and sometimes wrote. She worked hard at the theatre, invited the press to meet Eugène Ionesco for tea on the porch of a Victorian hotel and drove him all the way to Boston for a TV interview.

And then, she's standing in the bedroom with L, gesturing toward the shelf of radical books. A week after he leaves comes Hurricane Camille: 259 dead, Mississippi, Alabama,

Louisiana. She writes a poem in which she is Camille: destroyed coast, all the houses lost, people wandering ruins looking for one another.

Was this how a self felt?

The band is smoking pot, fumes through the house; she gives a big party and red wine stains the carpet.

In the dog days of August, she asks the producer if she can leave her job early: I'm having a nervous breakdown, she says. The producer is paying attention. She sends the lonely young woman to a psychiatrist at the local sanitarium, a very nice man. Did she mention to him that she was dropping out of the school? That she wanted to write?

She goes to the Adirondacks to take refuge with her family and learns of her mother's dissatisfaction, a rift in her parents' marriage. She is angry at her mother, worried for her father, who had been taken by surprise. She is taken by surprise. She had thought she had a perfect family. She had thought she was moving to Chicago to live with L, but when she finally reached him by phone, he told her he didn't want her to come. She moved alone to New York City.

I didn't think about *I'm having an abortion*, I just did it. Blasted through fear: I want this life, not that life. Rabbit test, rabbits leaping, more and more of them. The Friedman test was developed in 1931 to detect pregnancy. A woman's urine is injected into an immature female rabbit; after a few days, the animal is dissected; if her ovaries are enlarged, the woman is pregnant. Whatever the case, the rabbit dies.

Once in Wyoming, a small rabbit at the door: Muffy! The next day, two. Muffy and Buffy. The next day, three. Muffy, Buffy, Tuffy. This went on until I came to the end of the alphabet, a multitude of rabbits at my doorstep—they delighted me. *Autumn that year / Was a rabbit affair*: Velimir Khlebnikov (Russian, 1885–1922). There are rogue years when rabbits reproduce in multitudes.

My administration teacher, the assistant manager of the Metropolitan Opera, called me into his Lincoln Center office. If you want to write, he said, quit the drama school and go into psychotherapy. Something about me, he seemed to be saying, was more serious than the toys-in-his-office doctor understood.

I was stunned that this man with a heavy Bronx accent who told stories about opera divas and orchestra strikes had actually summoned me to Manhattan to advise me on my life.

I think of certain women, often very accomplished, maybe with one or two children, who cook for a dozen effortlessly.

Pasta. Salad. Then back to her studio in the afternoon. I first did amatriciana, then plain with garlic and oil, often with very thin slices of hot pepper. At an artists' colony in Umbria, eating supper under an arbor, I imagine myself that kind of woman.

Abortion, he says, how unattractive. He is in his forties.

I need to understand the science, I tell her, and some history. A mutual friend had introduced us, a doctor, by coincidence a college classmate of mine whom I hadn't known. She has committed her life to maternal health, the health of women, to finding a simple way to terminate a pregnancy. In the wake of the new feminism, a movement of women doctors, organizers, of medical professionals, international, worked in rural clinics all over the "developing world" educating women about their bodies, reproductive health, abortion.

There is a story from the early 1980s in India, she tells me, of an Indian gynecologist saying something like, There should be a pill for this.

As it happened, French scientists were developing one, a two-stage process that became known as a "medical abortion."

A study was undertaken, protocols developed, Institutional Review Board permissions procured—eventually the pills—thousands—were transported by hand.

The new method of abortion soon became widely available to women in India.

Conception is not a scientific word, it's a religious word, she says. How could I not have thought of this? Sunday after Sunday for my entire childhood, My soul doth magnify the Lord, and my spirit has rejoiced in God, my savior—this, the Virgin Mary in gratitude for her pregnancy.

In the fluid of the womb, she goes on, making circular gestures with her hands. It is not instant. It takes hours for the sperm to move, even get to the womb, where it will wander, meander for days, eventually finding an egg, then perhaps a day after that piercing and lodging within the egg wall, to form a zygote.

Days?

It could take as long as ten days. The point is, no one can say, for sure, when conception takes place.

Wow, I'm thinking.

It's a process, she says, from sex on.

Patiently, she explains the science of the abortion pill: progesterone to keep the fertilized egg from adhering to the uterine wall, four more pills to induce contractions to expel it. In the United States, in the early days only in the presence of a doctor, but now available directly to women, over the Internet and by mail.

Taking the pills at home by yourself has been found to be just as safe as taking them under supervision, she continues. Researchers had tested fourteen Internet sources—no fraud. In Europe you take it when you find you are late—even after missing just one period. Over the counter. Pregnancy termination in the hands of women.

Termination. I like the valence of the word, from the Latin *terminare*, to mark an end, or boundary, somehow free of the wreckage and pain, the fraught history of the word *abortion*.

You would not have had to have the operation, she says.

A man I once knew told me I'd make a wonderful mother, and slip-on-the-ice told me the first thing he'd do if we were together would be to knock me up. I slipped on ice, and he said hello. My dream of him—white houses on a narrow street, powder-blue door, sleeping infant—his of me, *knocked up*.

In the 1590s, slang for *brothel* was "knocking-shop." In nineteenth-century America, the asking price for an enslaved woman was "knocked up" if she was pregnant.

I n the parallel life, one September evening, I have dinner with my son who doesn't yet have a name in this story. He is almost thirty, but he seems that night like a child, looking at me with longing. I don't want to lose connection with you, he says. This takes me aback as I hadn't thought our connection ever at risk.

I lean closer.

Let's do our hand-holding thing, I say and reach for his, my hands on his at the center of the table, and we sit like that. This is when he says, Mama, I want to know why you didn't have me, which brings me to tears. I wanted all I hadn't lived, but without displacing anything I have lived. Johnny—there, he has a name—it's from *Rise and Fall of the City of Mahagonny* (Bertolt Brecht, Kurt Weill, 1930), which L was translating that fall we lived in the Chelsea—I'm thinking now of "Surabaya Johnny," a woman's slippery voice. I like the strange word—a city in Indonesia!—the dreamy off-kilter music.

Can I tell my son who has never known his father that I wouldn't have wanted the photographer's child?

My friend is in grief and we haven't seen each other in a year, an accidental hiatus. Her oldest, closest friend had died, the man who had been her mentor. It had been difficult to find a restaurant at the last minute, so we ended up at a place that was a bit ordinary—she was sick of our usual, Italian and farther up Lexington Avenue. We are both single, though she is a mother and divorced, a novelist. Also, she is ten years younger than I am, effectively a different generation.

I differ from most people on abortion, she says. She had asked what I was writing, and when I told her, went on to tell a story about getting pregnant a third time, when her second child was small, and how she hadn't wanted another but also didn't want an abortion. Her gynecologist said something to the effect of the dilemma being in God's hands, maybe she'd have a miscarriage, and that is what happened.

I wouldn't have had an abortion, she said. People identify either with the unborn child or with the mother. I identify with the unborn child.

It was my first autonomous decision, I said, unsettled by her declaration. That's what I'm writing about.

You were autonomous when you slept with the man who got you pregnant. She says this as a challenge. Almost hostile, which I know because my chest seizes, and my mind does that thing again, pieces of thinking clanging against one another, making what has been clear, blur and fog.

The next day I got an email—lovely that we'd moved on after the start of the evening, which she'd found *scratchy*—was it the exchange about autonomy that was *scratchy*? I'd felt humiliated when I said I identified with the woman. An old sickly embarrassment, accusation that

I am selfish. But the exchange spurred me to think through why I disagreed with her.

When L and I made love, I was not alone, because we wanted each other. With the photographer it was different—when he mounted me, which is what he did, I was unable to protest, as if anything I might say had gone out of me, drained out of me. I was acted upon. We had been drinking scotch.

My abortion was an action I undertook alone. I told the psychiatrist with toys in his office I would go crazy if I had a child. I did not know what other reason to give; I had no profession—was there any valid reason I couldn't be a mother? I just knew I did not want to be a mother. I wanted to figure out another kind of life.

I am frightened of argument, but I can usually represent myself.

I identify with the unborn child, my friend repeats as if I have not heard her.

And I, I say, I identify with the woman.

At seventy-seven, the most crucial medications I take every day are two kinds of eye drops for glaucoma; the doctor has said in no uncertain terms that I must not miss a day, so I set two alarms with five minutes in between to remind myself. The consequence of disobedience here is loss of sight. The optic nerve is not retrievable.

Sometimes I decide my optic nerve will regenerate (a scientific impossibility) and willfully skip the drops for a day or two. Why did I skip the pill? That same defiance? How often? Maybe I was hung over. Maybe I'd spent two nights in a row with L and didn't take my pills with me, little plastic kit.

Was that an act of autonomy?

I have to be more precise. The actual decision: Something was heading toward me, a life that I didn't want, and I stopped it. I didn't ask anyone. No one took me into custody as a crazy woman; no one even noticed.

How can you identify with the unborn child, who is not yet a child, at the expense of identifying with yourself?

"The last May of the century," my poem says of another Upper East Side evening. It was the first time I'd had a drink with the final man I fell in love with—I was fifty-five and he was married. I fell for him. *I love your blue eyes.*

In dark blue, more blue than dark. The walls are fresco, a half moment of gold. The infant is already there. I have a notion I have given birth to this child in an earlier frame of the dream, stunned when he—yes, it is a boy, but not separate from me—rises from the crib and begins to walk into the enormous illuminated room. He was, I believe, naked,

with the roundness of putti, the cherubs that inhabit quat-
trocento Italian paintings, and dragging behind him, as if
it were a garment fallen off, a length of fabric, not silk, not
linen—otherworldly and creamy, a wide stripe of unfath-
omable crimson, then a rich blue—heraldic. And now he
is speaking, a few words, then waves, cataracts of words,
sentences then paragraphs, complete thought. I am amazed.

False etymologies: amazement is that I am freed from
a maze—the *A* from the Latin *ab*, out of. And *putti*, which
does not come from *putare*, Latin, to think.

The second time I have the dream, I am nowhere present—
I am not the mother, and he is closer to an emanation.
I recognize him in the upward movement of his walk, the
pouring out of word and thought. I both hear and do not
hear, not the loss of dream memory I am accustomed to, but
silent, like an early black-and-white film, but the movement
smooth and the color true to life.

Forty years ago at a New York gala dinner at the Carlyle
Hotel, I was seated next to two distinguished older psychia-
trists who were married to each other. The woman was wearing a necklace of large pearls, real. (They had collaborated on
best-selling books about relationships.) We got to talking and
I told them I was single and a poet who also wrote nonfiction.
I felt a little embarrassed—I was in the presence of married
psychoanalysts who were, if not Freudian, something close

to it—and I had no "relationship." And then I told them that dream. Both exclaimed that I was really fine, that they were happy for me, and that when I married, I should invite them to the wedding and she would give me the string of pearls.

I consider again that there is no daughter in my dreams. Again ask if it is that my imagination has no room for a woman other than myself? Or is it that I have found living the life of a woman difficult? I remember, when I had my first male lover after years with women, encountering an older, very witty gay man who was a friend. He was a writer of high intelligence and great achievement and though I kind of loved him, he scared me. I hear you've found a man, he said, as if I had been rescued. I didn't even know he knew I'd been with women. Somehow the conversation led to my saying, I enjoy being a girl, and he said, I know.

Why no daughter? my friend asks. Her seventeen-year-old granddaughter figure skates to be alone, leaping across the silvery ice. What would I tell her about life?

VIII

Fallen but Also Aloft

A taint of accusation hovers when I write about sexuality: She's had bad relationships, they say. Fallen woman, the woman who sins, adulteress, slut, a stitch dropped from the fabric of society.

I didn't sleep with him, she said. I wanted him to marry me, and a man like that will not marry a woman he beds before marriage.

Sure, I'll sleep with you, but divorce your wife first, she said. He did and they are still married.

I wasn't interested in the Virgin in pale blue and white, sitting there with a baby on her lap. I wanted the red and purples of Magdalene, even the ravages, as in the unnerving sculpture of her in the duomo in Florence, haggard, carved from wood by Donatello (1453–55).

She fell into pleasure, too much ice cream. The smooth textures of ice cream, a moment of transcendence.

Fallen only in the imagination of patriarchs, who turn away from her humanness, and from their own. Does a man fail when he allows himself a woman's tenderness? We were children, two white bodies in a college room, Mahler on the record player, we were mining each other, we fell together, we shook and cried out, we clung to each other, we laughed and we were frightened and delighted.

Falling into red, of the crimson ceremony of blood, the red of Hester's *A* (Nathaniel Hawthorne, *The Scarlet Letter*, 1850) bursting its strictures, a circle of women talking. Healing, not reentry into polite society. With others raped and maligned, the fallen woman holds.

Scratched and bruised shin, a little blood. I'll act as if it didn't happen.

Fallen but also aloft. Across the middle of her abdomen a dark-gray likeness of a tenement block, windows. Interruption of red. Lights on.

It's a painting (Louise Bourgeois, *Fallen Woman*, 1946–47).

By the time I started to have sex, the idea of a fallen woman was obsolete, an antiquated figure of speech. Women, we ourselves, pulled her up from the dirt. We wanted to have sex.

When she is upright, when you are upright, when I am upright: walking and the shoe catches on the cement curb. Careen, fall, a hard landing. I did not break myself. I have never broken myself, tempting fate to say it.

Fallen Woman, in French *Femme Maison*, rectangular, horizontal, maybe six feet, three deep, the figure of a woman reclining, suspended in a red sky. In the painting, she flies the sky of red, bloodred: fallen but also aloft.

I reject enclosure, I call for the vividness of her beauty, I call for wisdom and the body's pleasure, I call for the red shriek of her transcendence.

The painter was in her nineties when I met her. Or was it the intensity of her eyes in a photographic portrait? No, I see her in black, I reach for her hand as friends introduce us.

What color lipstick did I wear then? Certainly not red. I had started to make up my eyes. I have a round face, always trying to make it look oval, so heavy eye makeup.

In the movie, Judy Garland, wearing white, strides out of Grand Central Station in a crowd, pulling herself up to her full height, a triumphant smile across her face. It's a wartime movie (Vincente Minnelli, *The Clock*, 1945) and she's met a soldier in for leave—trips over him on her way up a set of public stairs, heel comes off her shoe. He retrieves it, they find a shoemaker, a day and night in New York. When she gets home her roommate warns her about the soldier—no one knows who he is. Romance is framed as self-realization, an accident that becomes a means to finding her self. Such a cliché.

A self is a thing you are looking for. First in contradiction to others. My mother wore Raven Red, a dark lipstick. In the movie Judy Garland wears dark lipstick, her mouth almost black in the black-and-white film.

By the time I started wearing lipstick, movies were in color. My aesthetic was always the natural look, so I didn't venture far from my actual lip color, which I like. Until now, when I find that a slash of red across my face erases years, even decades, or so I imagine.

When at the end of the movie, Judy Garland pulls herself up to her full height and walks, it is as if she has not walked before.

The problem is, what comes after.

The thing that kept me outside looking in became a silence I choked on.

Hour exams, they kept saying. Early November, I think. I have to study for my hour exams, said the girl in black tights, the girl from Chicago Lab School, the girl from Milton Academy. What was an hour exam? At my public high school, there was no such thing. There was a nice older girl in the dorm, a senior, and I asked if she would talk to me. I went to her room and I said, I am really scared. What is an hour exam? I am afraid I am going to flunk.

They lose each other in the subway, Judy Garland and Robert Walker, and they don't know each other's last names! (Those crowds in the subway when you feel you're in a washing machine, and definitely if you are a sock the other one gets lost.) Eventually they find each other, the reunion so tense and desperate they fall into each other's arms, she says I can't be separated from you, he proposes, she accepts. Obstacles, obstacles, obstacles, but they marry at city hall. She: There were no flowers. Weeps. They walk, zombies, down some dark New York avenue, a pair of newlyweds bursts past them, rice, blossoms, cheering friends and family. They go into a church—"Saint Faith, Episcopalian"—it's empty and late at night. They read the marriage ceremony to each other from the prayer book. Consecrate on their own.

I hardly remember making love with L, though I did so many times in that turreted apartment across from the school. In the dark.

Before L, there was the first lover, and we were awkward. Then the director who said stop looking like a French movie. There was the white-bodied boy, to Mahler. There was the philosopher who knew how to touch me, but, as I now remember it, with a kind of disinterest I couldn't name then. The drama school boy, the summer theatre lighting designer who fucked like a scientist experimenting. And the one whose chest hair frightened me.

By the time I met L, I was curious about the expressive poem of sex—no, that's affected—the topography of a man's body and of my own. Summer of 1968, LP playing several feet from the tiny bedroom where I slept with the summer lighting designer, wild distortions of melody, a young white woman, an almost unbelievable voice (Laura Nyro, 1947–97).

How privileged I was and how unconscious. I remember walking up York Street on the way to the school with my friend Alan and his telling me he had taken a job as an orderly in

the hospital. Why, I said, thinking that he was researching
something he was writing. I need the money, he said. My
acupuncturist had to quit violin lessons in his teens because
he couldn't afford the teacher's fee, seventy-five cents. My
friend Lucy had to borrow a typewriter in college—she
couldn't afford her own. These lacks were beyond my under-
standing when I was twenty-three, though I did know the
inheritance I had by then made me unusual. I thought money
lasted forever.

My father's mother was philanthropic, guilty to the point
of panic about what she had. For my father the money was
a burden, which made him profligate. I have no memory of
the financial aspect of my abortion. The figure of $2,000
comes up ($16,000 now), but can that be true?

I have no memory of what came after the abortion except
that the two friends visited and brought me a sandwich.

In June before the Berkshires, I went to California. My friend
Pam had a part in a play called *Ceremonies in Dark Old Men*
(Lonne Elder, 1969). Did I stay with her? We were close then,
she out of school and making her way. I remember lying in
the sun while she was at rehearsal, reading Emma Goldman's
Living My Life (1931), the original two-volume hardcover,
its thrilling fusion of the erotic and radical politics. We used

the word *passion*. I read so intently I got sun poisoning, the scars on my chest still make me think of Red Emma.

The book is not just about my abortion.

I should hope not, he declaims. From the other man at the table, authentic interest. It's the summer of the Supreme Court decision, 2022. Why are we not in the streets? he says, as if it were my task to get us there.

I march, but I do not organize marches. I carried my eighty-seven-year-old friend the entire length of the women's march of 2017.

I wish to be accorded the privileges of a protagonist.

I had a friend once who had prophylactic breast surgery because her entire family had died of cancer. I feel pure, she said. Like a boy. It scares me how relieved I feel. She had a small smile that carried a lifetime of ennui—so much borne in silence that she died alone of a heart attack.

An image from nowhere: myself crawling, angry, blood red.

A bright-blue swatch of car, a bright-white swatch of oper-ating room, a swatch of gray, the recovery room. Who knew you were such a wild girl. Swatch of shame. Swatch of my future—if the past were the future: there's a pill for that. Right after the photographer. Right when I put my hands to my belly in that sunny room.

"I loved sex," says my poem much later (1992), the poem about the photographer. "It's hard to tell the truth. I / wanted to love sex."

Twitch and sweat, ooze, no consciousness then of the layers of silence. Often if I declared myself, I was ridiculed. I got used to it. Bang on the glass wall. I want to figure this out. I was rescuing my body. The discomfort, the sweating, the itching, the sadness, the disappointment, the certainty I will not be desired: the silence becomes animated and rebellious, fierce and embodied, but also restrained, held back, encased, gagged. In a red Triumph, his hands beneath my clothing, sweat and itch become hurry. I assume he has no fear. I do not consider fear is the reason he does not speak to me the next day. Or ever. Twenty-five years later we meet again; begin a correspondence. "A crack in the old silence," says my poem (1989). An ecstatic day in Montreal. I could have slept with him that night, but I did not invite him in. And there are other regrets: the older man, the great poet; the waiter in the Indian restaurant; the young man in the café down the street from my therapist's office. I check out the guys with white hair now. The hatchet of my silence. Past fear vibrates at the core.

When I go into the room of happy good mornings, I am afraid I will slip on the slick shiny steps.

For a long time, my abortion was mine. Not a secret exactly, but I considered it mine and mine alone. Until decades later when a critic writing about a book of mine on another subject raised the issue: She glosses over her abortion, which is troubling, is how I remember her sentence. Why hadn't I considered the feelings of my lover, she asked. I had written about L in passing in the book she was reviewing, but not about the photographer, whom I treated in the 1992 poem—"Landscape, / he says. Sets aside Nikon."

It is as if each man, two separate acts, had produced a pregnancy and I'd had two abortions. Those who read the poem know about the photo session. Those who read my prose believe I became pregnant by L.

In the spring, L brought poets to the school, one of them a woman with long honey-blond hair, and a few guys. They sit on stools, audience in the dark, and read their poems. As if talking.

Oh, I said to myself, I have to write poems, but not like Andrew Marvell (1621–78). It seems I had a future all lined up. It comes to me now that I knew I was pregnant, because I can feel the self trying out the role of L's appendage. Had I found a way to have it? I'm avoiding the word *abortion*.

Termination. As in, I hereby terminate one part of my life and begin another. The poets on tall stools, the woman just my age, at ease and confident.

The violence, if you can call it that, was to my body, but I do not call it that.

Why is my life story still bound to whether or not I have a child?

I didn't want that thing inside me, a friend in her sixties says with uncharacteristic force. She was married, but she had plans. Later, when she had a child, she wondered about the one she did not have.

I did not feel an intruding entity. What I said to myself was not *Get rid of it*, never *that thing*.

I was holding to reality as I knew it, as if the great magical world of my dreamed-up future were a vast glittering wall, in places opaque and blinking back, in places transparent, revealing vistas beyond. When I got the news that I was pregnant, it was as if the wall shuddered, were about to fall toward me and crush all I believed lay ahead of me, losing all illumination as it loosened from its foundations.

Run fast, little girl, outrun rabbits and doctors, outwit them thoroughly. It had more to do with luck and money than with wit. Always money. The gynecologist said he'd get her a psychiatrist and do it in a hospital, she says, for $1,800. A fortune! She was working three jobs just to stay in college.

There is a leak in the ceiling of my downstairs neighbor's kitchen, but upstairs in mine it was a torrent, almost an inch of water on the floor, warm as I had left it running. I had my earphones on so I couldn't hear until the week- end superintendent pounded on the door, raced into the kitchen and turned off the water, yanked everything from under the sink. I hauled out all my towels, threw them on the floor, soaked up the water and put them, sopping, drip- ping, drenched and heavy, into a garbage bag. I was bad; I was also embarrassed and ashamed—this time for being old. I'm sorry. I'm sorry. I'm sorry. This was the second time I'd done this in six months. Down to the basement to wash then dry the towels. The problem was that the basin in which I soaked dirty dishes blocked the drain. I ordered one with legs so water could flow under it, out the drain.

Leak, then a torrent of fury. I want to scrutinize what happened when I was twenty-three and how I moved forward. I am seventy-six. A jet overhead, and then so quiet you can hear a breeze through the trees, the distant caw of one crow.

IX

Horse, Woman, Snake

I no longer sit at a desk to write but pull out my laptop and begin. In New York, I do so in bed—Edith Wharton. Summers, on a sofa made ergonomic with cushions. In silence that resembles what I found the summer I was ten, reading myths, struck with wonder by the hard, beautiful face of a woman with snakes for hair.

When I say I speak with a woman's voice, I mean a self. I'm at the kitchen table and I am twenty-seven and writing. No other voice to drown me out.

Comes 24 June in the year 2022. The US Supreme Court: *Dobbs v. Jackson Women's Health Organization* (No. 19-1392, 597 US). Allow me numerology: digits of each unit of the date make six—two and four make six, the sixth month, and the three twos of the year also six. Three sixes,

666. In the Book of Revelations, the beast. In other texts, Antichrist, the devil.

A hard blank. Everything we did was for naught. In place, back in our place. In stone. What were we thinking, walking past those men in hard hats? We were young, talking and laughing. They looked at us, laughing, taking stock. By then we were free, our bodies free in New York State (1970). And our minds. You can't imagine the feeling, to be a young woman then. In a year our bodies would be free forever, all over America (*Roe v. Wade*, 1973).

I should have announced my freedom from enforced reproduction, celebrated with an orchestra, thunderous triumph: What will this young woman do with her life?

I was in my kitchen when my sister called. She had just had her fourth son. I won't have another, she said. She was thirty-six. I was forty. I know now that was the exact moment when I understood I would never have a child.

When I was ten, I began to read books about horses and to draw them. I drew horses wherever I was and on whatever sheet of paper I had. I drew them in the margins of books. When I got to college, I was still drawing them, flare of mane and tail, rearing on hind legs. Eventually I could draw an entire horse without lifting my pen or pencil from the surface. And then, out of the blue, I was drawing women, our hair and eyebrows, our lips. They were not self-portraits but essences.

My grandmother, who painted women more powerfully than she painted men, fell to pieces soon after she reached forty. When I was forty, I began to draw snakes. Why snakes? a friend asks. Something ancient, I tell her—in Greek mythology, regeneration, transformation. I drew their forked, darting tongues. Why is the tongue forked? The woman with blank eyes in the book of myths has hair of snakes but her snakes have no tongues.

Silence? No, let's say quiet, which does not imply enforcement.

An amaryllis blooms, stalk appearing with leaves, pale green and vertical and at the end of it, long buds, color of bloom through elongated, translucent envelopes, and then one morning it begins to open and the next day, a flower in the early light.

I am in a car with my father driving, and somehow the idea of a phallic symbol has come up. We often had these earnest conversations. I must be eleven or twelve, and I had never seen an erect phallus. Why, I ask, must any long thing be called a phallic symbol?

Not snakes but the serpent; in the garden the creature offers the young woman a way out, out of the lie of her origin in a man's body. She can enter charged quiet with a woman or a man, a woman/man or a man/woman. An other.

I have a second cup of coffee, not a good idea but I often do this now, forget in the present not to do something that will disrupt the future.

Choice. I prefer the word *decision*, its etymology containing ancient words for strike down, slay, stab, cut. But the syllable also occurs in *incisor*, the cutting tooth. It is the privilege to be incisive that has been taken away.

I began writing this eighteen months before the leak of the Supreme Court decision, which occurred on May 2, 2022. I was trying to get to the heart of the matter.

Shift: I am writing for the young women and also for the young men, for those of you who are silent, and today that includes me.

Write anything, something: The towel is striped, draped over the edge of a laundry basket. A lampshade. All white, nothing to describe. Or, small and angled, of creamy pale silk on a wire frame, curved out with sculpted sections like a peeled orange or an amaryllis just before blossom.

We were three young women in our twenties walking against the traffic, up Seventh Avenue. Somewhere between Fourteenth and Twenty-Third Street, we pass one of those Irish bars. We must have been beautiful, so young in our miniskirts or blue jeans.

I was very young for twenty-three. Just look at that face. We were more than bodies, I am thinking, but what an irony since I first understood freedom through my body—what is not physical comes from the physical. Thought, idea, belief. I cannot decide on one word. Is there a word that is entirely my own?

Observe the conversion of the saint on the road to Damascus—an encounter with disembodiment and he falls to his knees in recognition. Split of consciousness. Recognition not of God outside himself but of an emanation so powerful it cannot be contained by the body.

My God, I hear myself say. Not God, says the lover, whose hands pull me open. It's you.

Sixth Avenue goes up, and I am walking down. There is a woman ahead of me pushing a stroller with her child in it; for the first time I am aware of a mother younger than I am. I was twenty-six, writing and beginning to publish. You weren't a very good writer, a woman from the past says decades later, but you are now. Did I smile and thank her for retracting the insult she'd never delivered?

I have five sisters and all of them have children.

One summer in the Adirondacks with my sisters, each with a baby on her hip or by the hand, I see it: your body is no longer your own. Extreme beauty vanishes into the sound of their want. Often, in spite of myself, I can feel bereft, left out of something. It's not that I didn't intend to have children, I try to explain, it's that I never *wanted* to have children.

I do not remember when my choice became a decision.

I began to draw women. Their heads, their faces, following the line my hand made. How fast can I get a face? Their hair was always long—rebuke to my mother, who cut mine short.

Don't take your hand from the pen or the pen from the page. Woman after woman. The one I just drew has a scribble for a mouth—the next is serious, looking off to the left. I always begin with the left eye—my own left eye sees less well.

Wrench the woman to the center of her circumstances. Was it shut up, shut up, shut up that shook me to life, or was it the first pen I picked up?

Alone in that small room, I read the myths. Diana, Aphrodite, Athena, and Demeter whose daughter Persephone is abducted by Pluto, god of the underworld. Grief of winter. Danaë, raped by Zeus, gives birth to a son, Perseus. Women with children and without. Women in jeopardy whom goddesses protect. One grieves. Another is turned into a white heifer, another is the daughter of the river god. Another becomes a tree. I like seeing women within trees, a woman running a race against men, stories of golden apples, of a goddess who kills a boar.

Virgin, Magdalene, Martha, and the other Mary, who will not help her sister serve at table. As a girl in church, my imagination took to Magdalene not because she sat with ointments at the feet of the wounded god, but because she was drawn by desire. I do not yet know that early texts tell us she was the thirteenth apostle. Mary, the sister who would not do the dishes.

I turn a page to the hard beautiful face of a woman with snakes for hair. In the myth, the snakes hiss, but in my ten-year-old imagination they are silent, their movement sensual. When I begin to draw snakes, I draw them at rest, also the slinking gesture of their bodies extending.

Snake as transformation, but also regeneration. Motion is what matters, rather than the thing in motion. I draw the snake and I see what I have drawn—not something to fear. The moment in translation when a word, suspended between one language and another, exists free of language. An object falls from my hand—the moments in space before it reaches the floor.

In the book, she has no color, but they say the Greeks painted their sculptures. Snakes as green, as red, as azure and orange. The snake hair was a punishment, it is said, for her tryst with Apollo. Radiance. Perseus is told that if he looks at her face he will turn to stone. There is no myth of a young woman looking at the woman with snakes for hair, of a young woman who resists turning to stone.

I am standing here, on an outcropping of granite. Abruptly the sun is overshadowed and there is a harsh chill in the air, seconds ago so pleasant. Let's say I am outside time but within a dimension of time that includes all I have lived. I am considering what has been forbidden and also the idea of consequences. I am often here with my sisters, but today I am alone.

I hear the snakes curling and uncurling. A sound like the words *sheathe*, *hush*, *streak*, *expanse*. Because I can see her with my back to her, I evade the curse.

Was it she I was looking for when I opened the outdoor entrance to the cellar and went in? So literal, thinking I would find some secret of the past in the cellar beneath that childhood room. I do not want to reduce her to what I imagine she might say. Reduce her, Medusa. Slant rhyme.

What is it that remains unsaid?

At a table in late autumn, I make my way through what I have written here. Interesting how I can't remember the beginning when I reach the end. It's always that way, how you're tossed forward to start again.

I did not tell, begins this book.
   I'm telling you, ends the long-ago poem.

—NEW YORK CITY, 2020–22

Acknowledgments

There are four people without whom this book would not exist, and I thank them beyond measure: Sarah Chalfant, who said yes, do it. Mary Allen, for remote fast writing sessions, NYC / Iowa City. The never-wavering Robert Leleux, for reading and rereading. Brigid Hughes: for *seeing* this book and its author, for her uncanny insight, meticulous attention, and respect for the traditions and enterprise of literature.

A book comes from the efforts of many, and they are how a book moves into the world. They are also first readers. For all of you, no thanks is sufficient: Ruby Wang of A Public Space; Anne McPeak, redemption through copyediting; Janet Hansen for the cover design that reminds me boldness is good; Francesca Richer for the elegant interior design;

Kait Astrella, remarkable publicist, and Katie Freeman, for getting the word out. Alyssa Shea, for making the book presentation visual, and Michelle Roque, web designer extraordinaire. And forever thanks to Rebecca Nagel, Bonnie McKiernan, and everyone at the Wylie Agency.

For their memories, perspectives, time, and thinking, thank you: Beverly Winikoff, Marina Warner, Quito Ziegler, Jill Eikenberry, Heather Domenicis, Ellen Chesler, Sherry Turkle, Robert Mandel, Pamela Diamond, Peg Boyers, Daphne Merkin, Mary Gordon, Michael Posnick, Gordon Talley, Robert Fowler, Barbara Smith, Victoria Redel, Jim Hart, and Pamela Jones (a.k.a. Revalyn Gold), whom I was unable to locate.

Gratitude for support in the past as I remembered, and in the present as I wrote and sought a place for this book: Robert Boyers, Laura Cronk, David Freeman, Charles Dillingham, Rita Gabis, Carol Gilligan, Vivian Gornick, Margo Jefferson, Elizabeth Kendall, Herman Krawitz, Adrian Nicole LeBlanc, Claire Messud, Marian Moore, Rosemary Moore, Laila Nabulsi, Robert Polito, Victoria Redel, Luz Rivera, Susan Robertson, Max Rudin, Jennifer Cho Salaff, Maggie Simmons, the students and faculty of the New School writing program, and those whom I may have not remembered—please forgive me.

And for conversations I had with women during the writing of the book: What are you writing about? *My pre*-Roe *abortion*. I had one. . . . and then I would get a story, which (startlingly) often concluded with the woman saying, You are the first person I've ever told.

In memoriam, with gratitude: Lily Farmer and Gordon Rogoff.